The Laurel Shakespeare

Each play is presented in a separate volume handsomely designed to incorporate these special features:

THE TEXT is a modern restoration of the original folios completed in late 1958 by *Charles Jasper Sisson,* Assistant Director and Senior Fellow at the Shakespeare Institute, Stratford-upon-Avon.

THE FORMAT designed for this volume employs the largest and most readable type available in any popular edition of the plays.

THE MODERN COMMENTARY by actors, directors and critics recently associated with the respective plays offers an authoritative insight into a special aspect of the play. *Esme Church* has been a leading lady at the Old Vic, where she has also directed a number of modern classics, as well as Shakespearean plays, among them AS YOU LIKE IT.

THE INTRODUCTION by the General Editor, *Francis Fergusson,* University Professor of Comparative Literature at Rutgers, provides dramatic and critical background.

SHAKESPEARE AND HIS THEATRE, also by *Professor Fergusson,* presents the known facts of Shakespeare's life and dramatic career along with a description of the Globe company.

THE GLOSSARY NOTES, especially prepared for this volume by *H. H. Smith,* Cornell University, define Elizabethan terms and special allusions not found in desk dictionaries.

The Laurel Shakespeare
Francis Fergusson, General Editor

As You Like It

by William Shakespeare

Text edited by Charles Jasper Sisson

Commentary by Esme Church

CONTENTS

Introduction by the General Editor

As You Like It was probably written in 1599, which would make it the next to the last of Shakespeare's great romantic comedies. As Shakespeare tells us in the title, he devised it to please his large and diversified popular audience. He put in something for every taste, from the subtle, idealized love of Rosalind and Orlando to Touchstone's anti-romantic affair with his Audrey; and he brought the many amusing complications of the story to the end which all good comedies must have: marriage for nearly everybody, with laughter and music. It is all warmed and lighted by Shakespeare's own holiday mood, which is both mocking and gentle; many readers think it the most perfect of his light, poetic entertainments.

He took the plot (as confecters of modern musical comedies so often do) from a popular novel, Lodge's *Rosalynde* (1590). He makes the story clearer and swifter than Lodge did, and he takes it much less seriously. Duke Frederick has usurped the dukedom of his elder brother ("Duke Senior"), who is living in exile with his loyal followers in the Forest of Arden. Frederick's daughter Celia and his brother's daughter Rosalind, childhood friends, are living at Frederick's court when the play opens. Sir Rowland de Boys' sons, Oliver the oldest and Orlando the youngest, are there too. The middle brother, Jaques (not to be confused with the "melancholy Jaques") is away until the end of the play. Oliver and Orlando quarrel, and Orlando has to flee for his life, but not until he and Rosalind have fallen in love. Duke Frederick banishes Rosalind too; Celia follows her; and all join Duke Senior in the Forest of Arden. It is in that pretty realm that the main business of the play—flirtations and mocking laughter—takes place. The plot is wound up when Oliver and Duke Frederick repent their wickedness, Duke Senior is restored to his dukedom, and all the young people get married.

Lodge's novel is "pastoral romance": that is, a tale of

somewhat Christianized shepherds and shepherdesses, nymphs and woodland gods, derived ultimately from Greek romances like those of Theocritus—the whole set in a beautiful country suggesting both Eden and the classical Golden Age. Since Dante, Europe had been fascinated with "pastoral." It is the basis of countless paintings, stories, early operas, masques and ballets, and also of much love-poetry. It is, of course, conventional and literary, but at its best it expresses the Renaissance delight in the world, and its idealized but sophisticated cult of human love. Shakespeare mixes with Lodge's romance several comic themes of his own invention, notably those of Jaques, Touchstone, Audrey, and William the country bumpkin.

Lodge's characters are rather colorless, but *As You Like It* is filled with those figures that live for us both on the stage and in our imaginations. Miss Esme Church, in her account of her production at the Old Vic, has explained how recognizable they all are to good actors. Shakespeare must have had English types in mind when he wrote them, and also the actors who would play them: a particularly talented boy-actor for Rosalind, for instance. The part of Touchstone was apparently written for Robert Armin, a professional jester and well-known personality in London. Much of the life and meaning of the play is in the characters, and there is no difficulty in enjoying them. The modern producer does, however, have a problem with the Forest of Arden and its romantic conventions, as Miss Church also points out: how is one to make that setting visible and acceptable on the modern stage? Miss Church solved this problem by staging the play in the style of Watteau, who recorded for Louis XIV the last appearance of the pastoral nymphs and shepherds in the palace park. The reader is referred to her essay. It throws much light on the play, which is at once "real" and the most playful make-believe.

The reader of course does not have to solve the technical problems of style, settings, and costumes. But the reader too must know a little about the manners, the poetic and theatrical conventions, and the popular ideas which Shakespeare used, if he is to enjoy the comedy and the poetry to the full. The characters are always making fun of their own romantic love-making; of the customs of the court; of the ideas current at the time. In their jokes and in their lyrics they build up the imagined scene, which is not to be taken too seriously, filled though it is with real feeling.

The first act is a prologue, in which Shakespeare quickly sets forth the basis of the plot. The first scene moves like a simple adventure-story: Orlando and Oliver have their fight, and Oliver engages Charles the Wrestler to finish off his younger brother. But in scene two we meet Rosalind and Celia, and their leisurely joking shows us what the main action of the play will be. "Let me see," says Rosalind, "what think you of falling in love?"

> CELIA
> Marry I prithee do, to make sport withal. But love no man in good earnest, nor no further in sport neither than with the safety of a pure blush thou mayst in honour come off again.

That well describes Rosalind's delicate "sport" with Orlando, which will occupy her, in the Forest of Arden, till love overcomes her fears. But at this point she does not know Orlando, and Celia suggests the alternative pastime:

> Let us sit and mock the good housewife Fortune from her wheel, that her gifts may henceforth be bestowed equally.

Since the middle ages Fortune had been personified as a goddess who turned her wheel, raising one man and lowering another, without regard to justice. She distributed the world's goods according to her whim, especially in cities, and in courts like Frederick's, where all were intriguing for power and money. Celia wants to blame Fortune for making honest women (among whom she counts herself, no doubt) "ill-favouredly"; but Rosalind says Nature is to blame for that. They continue the theme of Nature and when Touchstone appears, call him a "natural"—that is, a born idiot.

Everyone knew that Touchstone was played by Robert

Armin, a very intelligent man; and everyone could see that
Rosalind and Celia were both "honest" and "fair." The
girls are only joking, like timid young people in any period;
half-ironically blaming Fortune for a world they never
made; half-secretly longing for love, and hoping that Nature
has made them honest and fair enough for the right love—
which, of course, would cure everything. But the notions of
Love, Fortune, and Nature, which they start here, echo
throughout the lyrics and the play of wit in the Forest of
Arden. Soon Rosalind and Celia will flee there, abandoned
by Fortune; and there they will find Nature, and test, in
their flirtations, their natures and those of their lovers.

The climax of Act I comes in scene three, when Orlando throws the redoubtable Charles, knocking him out
and breaking a few ribs in his enthusiasm. At the same time
he and Rosalind (as they both remark) are "thrown" by
each other's charms. Orlando's victory offends the Duke
and makes him suspect Rosalind, who flees with Celia and
Touchstone. So we are prepared for the main business of
the evening in the Forest of Arden.

The Forest of Arden is first described by Charles (Act I,
Scene 1) as the place where the exiled Duke lives with his
followers "like the old Robin Hood of England"; there they
all "fleet the time carelessly as they did in the golden world."
Shakespeare wanted the Forest to suggest the Golden Age
of pastoral romance; but he does not hesitate to put the
Greenwood Tree there, palms among the beechs, and a lion
among the English sheep. He does not take any of these
romantic settings too literally; he plays with them, in order
to suggest a delightful state of mind, a vacation from the
cares of the world. "Are not these woods/ More free from
peril than the envious court?" says Duke Senior (Act II,
Scene 1). Even the winter winds, out here, are morally good
for us: "counsellors/ That feelingly persuade me what I
am." He has, of course, lost his dukedom through Fortune's
whim, but "Sweet are the uses of adversity," for they leave
us plenty of time to philosophize.

Shakespeare expects us to smile at Duke Senior's middle-
aged enthusiasm for the country (like that of a city-man

who has just moved to the suburbs); but we must agree with Amiens, who remarks:

> Happy is your Grace
> That can translate the stubbornness of Fortune
> Into so quiet and so sweet a style.

Duke Senior, in fact, shows us the Forest of Arden as it is for all his followers.

The "melancholy Jaques" is an even more tireless moralizer than Duke Senior, and soon (Act II, Scene 7) he reports that he has found a kindred spirit in Touchstone:

> I met a fool,
> Who laid him down and basked him in the sun,
> And railed on Lady Fortune in good terms,
> In good set terms, and yet a motley fool.

These three characters, in their railing at Fortune, play many humorous and poetic variations on popular philosophic notions of the time. Thus Jaques, teased by Duke Senior (Act II, Scene 7), gives a classic defense of the satirist's right to "speak his mind" and cleanse the world, provided he mentions no real individuals. When Orlando in the same scene breaks in on their picnic and, with his sword drawn, demands food, Duke Senior mildly remarks:

> Thou seest, we are not all alone unhappy.
> This wide and universal theatre
> Presents more woeful pageants than the scene
> Wherein we play in.

That starts Jaques off on his famous speech, "All the world's a stage." This idea was often heard in the Renaissance; Shakespeare himself touches upon it in several of his plays. Jaques combines it here with another familiar piece of popular wisdom, that of the Ages of Man. The result is that humorous and rueful little poem which everyone recognizes. The philosophizing of Jaques is closely akin to Amiens's beautiful songs: variations, touched with Shakespeare's genius, on old and standard themes. It is evident that Jaques enjoys his "melancholy" hugely. In our time only sophomores have enough leisure to indulge in their pessimistic "bull sessions," but for the Elizabethans mulling over the problems of man and Fortune seems to have been a favorite pastime. Duke Senior and his followers, too old for romantic love, are confirmed addicts of that game.

But flirtation was more exciting than philosophy then, as it is now; and that sport begins when Rosalind, Celia and Touchstone reach the Forest of Arden (Act II, Scene 4). They are suitably dressed for the Golden Age: Touchstone in his motley, Celia as the "shepherdess" Aliena, and Rosalind as that pretty shepherd-boy Ganymede, who was Zeus's favorite in the old Greek story. The first people they meet are those very literary shepherds, Corin and Silvius. When Silvius utters the traditional complaint of the rejected lover, and runs off crying, "Phebe, Phebe, Phebe!" Rosalind and Touchstone both recognize their fates. Rosalind will put Orlando through all the romantic paces; but Touchstone will tackle the problem of Audrey without a trace of romance, for he has long since passed the time of sighs and blushes.

In pastoral romance the lovers must always be kept apart as long as possible, for the point is not love's fulfillment, but the mysterious, painful and Eden-like moment of love's first innocent revelation. Orlando and Rosalind-Ganymede, after their "fall" in Act I, do not meet again until Act III, Scene 2. Even then Rosalind is miraculously insulated from Orlando by the thin disguise of her boy's costume. That disguise served Shakespeare the actor-manager well, for of course Rosalind was played by a boy-actor. And it serves Rosalind too. She is able to keep Orlando at a distance, and at the same time (when she persuades him to practice his wooing on "Ganymede") she has the excitement without committing herself. It is the old game of flirtation, but Rosalind is not dishonest in this, for she suffers the pangs of love herself, and wearies Celia with her endless talk of Orlando. She is trying to make sure that Orlando loves her as much as he says he does, and as much as she loves him. She wants nothing less than the finest love of the Renaissance poets: innocent and free as Eden, but deep as faith.

She makes poor Orlando, in his wooing, adopt (or pretend) all the attitudes of the desperate romantic lover; but she makes fun of these conventions even while she uses them. She never loses her balance, and is perfectly capable of enjoying a bawdy joke now and then. In short, she sees almost all the "angles" of love in the Forest of Arden.

The wooing of Rosalind and Orlando alternates with Silvius's wooing of Phebe, and Touchstone's businesslike arrangements with Audrey. At the same time the older characters continue to play witty variations on Fortune, Love and Nature. Touchstone and old Corin, the court- or city-man and the country philosopher, slyly show up each other's delusions (Act III, Scene 2). Corin reveals Touchstone's artificialities, and Touchstone makes clear, with plenty of gory details, just what a messy business the breeding of sheep really is. All are enjoying their vacations in the Forest of Arden—or the Golden Age—yet making fun of that poetic creation at the same time. The effect is like a country dance, in which people of many different "natures" keep time together: some young, some old, some glamorous, some laughable. Rosalind and Orlando are at the center of the kaleidoscope; Silvius and Phebe offer a burlesque of the literary and romantic aspects of their love, while Touchstone and Audrey keep us reminded of biology.

The enjoyment of love or wit in the leisure of Arden is the business of the play, but we do not expect that idyllic season to last forever. And Shakespeare keeps us reminded of the plot by means of very brief scenes in Frederick's court. When the repentant Oliver reaches the Forest (Act IV, Scene 3), we realize that Fortune is turning her wheel again: she is smiling upon the exiles, and it is time for them to return, under these happy auspices, to the workaday world. The finale (Act V, Scenes 2, 3 and 4) is elaborate, like that of a hit musical in our own theatre; for each of the main characters must have a few lines and take a bow, before the audience goes home.

Rosalind tell us (Act V, Scene 2) that Oliver and Celia, the last of the lovers, have made up for lost time by a simultaneous case of love-at-first-sight: "they are in the very wrath of love, and they will together. Clubs cannot part them." As Ganymede, she takes charge of her affair with Orlando, and of Silvius's with Phebe. Each lover must affirm that he is "made of sighs and tears," and also of "faith and service"; and each must promise to abide by Ganymede's commands. This passage is as ceremonious as a children's game, when all the players, blindfolded, march trustingly to claim their prizes when the magic word is spoken.

Touchstone and his bewildered Audrey have an interlude (Act V, Scene 3) and the pages sing the beautiful song, "It was a lover, and his lass," to remind us of real country-wooing in the fields. Then (Act V, Scene 4) the rest of the cast begins to assemble, to hear Ganymede's mysterious decrees; and while "he" is offstage (to change his costume, no doubt) Jaques and Touchstone have a chance to make their final joking comments on the proceedings:

> JAQUES
> There is sure another flood toward, and these couples are coming to the ark. Here comes a pair of very strange beasts, which in all tongues are called fools.

Touchstone apparently agrees with him, for he describes his "beast," Audrey, without flattery: "an ill-favoured thing sir, but mine own." He proceeds to his mock-pedantic account of "quarreling by the book," which must have amused Shakespeare's audience vastly, for fashionable dueling was a standard joke, and Touchstone is probably referring to an actual book on the subject (*Vincentio Saviolo his Practice,* 1595). Then, at last, music announces the ceremonious entrance of Hymen, attendants, and Rosalind, now in her proper female attire. Hymen was the Greek god of marriage, Apollo's son, who adorned many a splendid wedding-masque in Shakespeare's time. He is the proper figure to preside over marriage in the Golden Age, with its mingling of classical and Christian feeling; and he takes the center of the stage long enough to sing of the ideal dream of marriage, "When earthly things made even/ Atone together"; that is, when they are made one in harmony.

Hardly has Hymen's moment ended in laughter at Touchstone and Audrey, when Jaques de Boys arrives to give the older exiles *their* prizes. Duke Frederick has turned from the world to religion, whither the melancholy Jaques will follow him; and Duke Senior is restored to his dukedom. It is melancholy Jaques who formally presents each one with his due, and then all "atone together" in the rhythm and harmony of the final dance. Rosalind, the most glamorous character, who has seen and enjoyed the most, speaks the epilogue.

Shakespeare, like Jaques, turned from this holiday entertainment to more sober concerns, for in the next six or seven years he wrote his great tragedies. He did not treat the pastoral themes again until his last plays, when that vision of innocence is part of a wider pattern which includes suffering and guilt. In *As You Like It* the Eden-like love of Rosalind and Orlando is seen in a purely comic context: that of the strange capers which all kinds of people fall into when love strikes them.

F. F.

SUGGESTIONS FOR FURTHER READING

The New Variorum Edition of the play (1890) (p. 182) contains the usual copious notes: Lodge's *Rosalynde* and the older *Tale of Gamelyn*, and a wide sampling of criticisms up to that time. Further criticisms of the play are in Goddard, Traversi, Van Doren, Clemen and Dean: *Shakespeare: Modern Essays in Criticism* (pages 181-182). Webster (page 180) discusses the play on the modern stage.

Narrative and Dramatic Sources of Shakespeare. Edited by Geoffrey Bullough. London and New York: 1958. Vol. II, *The Comedies.*

This volume contains Lodge's *Rosalynde,* and the older *Syr Clyomon and Clamydes.* The editor writes a valuable introduction on Shakespeare's use of his sources.

Barber, C. L. *Shakespeare's Festive Comedy.* Princeton: 1959.

Chapter 9 is an excellent analysis of *As You Like It* in
the light of recent scholarship and criticism.

Hotson, Leslie. *Shakespeare's Motley*. London: 1952.
A study of the Fools and Jesters of Shakespeare's time,
and an account of Robert Armin, who probably played
Touchstone. Useful for an understanding of that role.

A NOTE ON THE TEXT

The play was first printed in the Folio of 1623. The entry
in the Stationers' Register is accepted as a protective entry
against piracy. The Folio gives a clean text, which probably
represents a prompt-copy, and offers little difficulty. In
doubtful readings, the following have been adopted, or introduced: I. i. 1-2, it was upon this fashion bequeathed;
I. ii. 284, smaller; I. iii. 11, child's father; I. iii. 24, cry in
time; I. iii. 104, your change; II. i. 5, feel we not; II. i. 18,
Amiens. I would not change it; II. i. 50, friend; II. v. 51f.,
Jaques. Thus it goes. [*Gives a paper*.] *Amiens* [*sings*]. *If it
do come to pass* . . . ; II. vii. 73, the weary very means; III.
ii. 111, wintered; III. ii. 163, Jupiter; III. ii. 250, drops such
fruit; III. iii. 91, in the mind; but; IV. iii. 88, ripe forester;
V. ii. 104, observance.

In accordance with common usage the numbering of
lines, together with Act and Scene indications, follows as
closely as possible that of the Globe edition. Where no
stage directions in fact occur, this is indicated by square
brackets enclosing the stage directions.

Spelling is modernized. But there is no modernization of
the language as used by Shakespeare and his actors. The
elaborate apparatus of stage-directions, mostly dating from
eighteenth-century editors, is eschewed. Where the original
texts convey Shakespeare's own directions, of course they
must be respected, though not necessarily verbatim.

Professor Sisson has further revised the text of this
edition.

Commentary on the Watteau
"As You Like It," at the Old Vic

BY ESME CHURCH

"I'll tell thee Charles, it is the stubbornest young fellow of France." So says Oliver to Charles, the Wrestler, speaking of his brother. Nonsense! This can only be Shakespeare paying lip-service to the source of his play. Thereafter he throws away all pretense; we are in the Forest of Arden, lying as it does in the heart of his childhood's Warwickshire, to the north of Stratford-upon-Avon, hiding amid its foliage some of the prettiest hamlets of this most English county.

Sir Arthur Quiller-Couch wrote of *As You Like It:* "He who knows Arden has looked into the heart of England and heard the birds sing in the green midmost of a moated island."

At the opening of the play we might be anywhere, the nobility and gentry have so much in common the world over. Yet even in the first scene we are face to face with a most English character, Adam the privileged family retainer; first played, according to tradition, by Shakespeare himself. This denial that we are in France confronts us throughout the play. The Usurping Duke, Oliver, Le Beau, could be French; witty, volatile Rosalind might be French; but Celia is all English and so is Touchstone. The Banished Duke and his followers, and above all, the "country copulatives," as Touchstone grossly names them, are pure Warwickshire drawn from the memory of the country boy whose mother was an Arden. They are the rich children of the English soil, forcing their way again and again into all his plays, no matter where he tells us the scene is laid!

Question therefore, where shall we set the play? We paid lip-service to the line about the young gentleman of France and the source of the story, and dressed the production in

the manner of the French artist Antoine Watteau; so that
at moments the stage looked like the Fête Champêtre and
Touchstone was Watteau's clown, Le Grand Gils, come to
life. The idea was suspect at first, and yet it had some justi-
fication. Shakespeare shows a fine disregard of time and
place in all his plays; Antoine Watteau shows a fine disregard of period in his costumes. An intimate friend of the
Court players, if he wanted a certain color he ransacked
their wardrobe until he found what he wanted, then used
it in his paintings. His pictures show us the French Court
playing at a day in the country. Shakespeare gives the same
kind of people playing at exile in the Forest of Arden;
Charles the Wrestler tells Oliver that they "fleet the time
carelessly as they did in the golden world." No less important is the question of girl turned boy, a problem which
Shakespeare's company with their highly trained boy-actors
did not have to concern themselves about. The Watteau
costumes flatter the feminine figure in boy's dress as no
other period does, and so Rosalind's change becomes cred-
ible. The audience must believe that Orlando thinks he is
laughing with a boy.

I had one other reason, a purely personal one. When,
some years before, I had played Rosalind at the Old Vic
(not very remarkably, I think), one of the London critics
commented that I had stressed the wit, "almost as though
Shakespeare had thrown off a Restoration comedy, in his
spare time. Not a bad idea!" The thought had stayed with
me, and when I found to my delight that Edith Evans was
to play Rosalind, well, what more suitable than that this
Queen of Restoration Comedy, this wittiest of actresses
should play it in Watteau, with all the manner she has at
her command. We were rewarded. She was superb, and the
critics praised generously.

The play is a romantic idyll and our aim is to induce the
audience to "fleet the time carelessly as they did in the
golden world." There are moments of danger which must
be given full value, so that the light moments may gain from
the shadows. Behind Rosalind, Celia and the Banished
Duke, lurks the menace of Duke Frederick. Oliver and

Charles must constitute a real danger to Orlando in the opening scenes of the play. The situation is clearly laid before us in Orlando's first speech to Adam. As in all fairy tales he is the youngest brother of three. Oppressed and deprived of his birthright, he decides to seek his fortune. Oliver enters and we are given a taste of his tyrannical moods. There is a fight between him and Orlando in which we see something of the strength and skill which make it possible for Orlando to defeat Charles in the next scene. The plot which Oliver hatches with Charles after the exit of Orlando may be petulant and bad-tempered, but it is real. Charles's threat against Orlando: "If he come to-morrow, I'll give him his payment. If ever he go alone again, I'll never wrestle for prize more. And so God keep your worship," is surely not a light thing. It is therefore very important to the play, to Rosalind and to Duke Frederick, that the wrestling should be exciting and dangerous. We must feel that the Duke's moody dismissal of Orlando is due to fear; another fine young fellow is ranged in allegiance against him. Frederick's hold on his people would seem to be tenuous; we have already been told of the Banished Duke that "many young gentlemen flock to him every day," and Le Beau strengthens this statement in the speech to Orlando in which he counsels him to fly. There follows at once Frederick's rash and violent banishment of Rosalind.

Twice more the violent element comes into the play: first when Frederick discovers that Celia has gone with Rosalind, and later when he confronts Oliver with his suspicions and dispossesses him of lands and living unless he apprehend his brother. This second scene is often omitted, since it is a cut back from the Forest of Arden and therefore presents scenic difficulties. We played it in the Orchard at night, with Duke Frederick and his "toughs" entering with lanterns, hunting Oliver down, which made it very sinister. After this Duke Frederick is seen no more, and is not even mentioned till the last scene of the play when Jaques brings the news of his intended raid upon his brother's camp, and unexpected conversion. However, we introduced the threat of his power on the entrance of Orlando into the Forest. The Duke and

his company were around their campfire at sunset, with the
foresters set as sentries. Orlando crept up behind one of
these men, disarmed and threw him down; the scene was
thrown into a confusion of drawn swords and startled cries,
and held for a tense moment before the Duke broke it with
his lines:

> Art thou thus emboldened man by thy distress?
> Or else a rude despiser of good manners,
> That in civility thou seem'st so empty?

The Duke did not move till this moment but his followers
had surrounded him in the firelight, with their weapons
drawn; the forester lay upon the ground and Orlando was
high above them all, upon a rock, sword in hand, threaten-
ing the second sentry.

All who come into the Forest of Arden are driven either
by adversity or the strong compulsion of their own natures.
Take them in order of their arrival. The Banished Duke,
too kindly and phlegmatic to allow his claim to the dukedom
to embroil his people in a petty civil war, has escaped from
the "perils of an envious court." His followers are voluntary outcasts, for his sake. Jaques is a born exile, wandering
forever in search of the reasons for man's life and actions.
The next to arrive are Rosalind and Celia; the first an innocent victim of fear and jealousy; Celia driven by her love
for Rosalind and disillusionment with her father. Touchstone is there because for Celia "He'll go along o'er the wide
world." What a picture the words conjure of the gentle fool
and the child, to be echoed in another play by the picture
of Yorick and the boy Hamlet. We find later how strongly
the country calls to Touchstone. Next to arrive are Orlando
and Adam; Orlando banished like Rosalind, while Adam follows him in "love and loyalty." Granville-Barker commented that the word "gold" was used more often in *The
Merchant of Venice* than in any other play. The word
loyalty is often used in *As You Like It,* an endearing quality
which gives much warmth to the play. The last to arrive is
Oliver; exiled and threatened, despoiled of lands and titles;
the victim of his own machinations, hoist with his own

petard! In Arden they all find their hearts' desire. Those who return go back the richer for their journey, and those who stay there are content.

All Shakespeare's plays are hard to cast. Exquisite snatches of poetry are put into the mouths of page boys; important situations are dominated momentarily by characters who appear for minutes only. One of the worst examples of this last difficulty is Duke Frederick. If he does not dominate the first few scenes of the play it deteriorates into the plodding prologue to a fairy tale; the audience is impatient for Arden, where the fun begins. But Frederick is a thankless part and few experienced actors are interested to play it. He should suggest a highly strung, self-willed introvert, on the edge of his nerves. Not without charm, his first words to Orlando are friendly, even kindly, changing in a flash when he hears his father's name. A man of unpredictable moods, he can threaten an unoffending niece with death, or turn "convertite" on an emotional impulse.

Oliver seems to me to be a reasonable picture of the kind of courtier such a man would attract; just as Le Beau, a time-server, smooth and watchful, is another. But Oliver must be aware of the dangers of his allegiance, and something of the explosive atmosphere of the court is partly accountable for his behavior to Orlando and the dastardly plot which he hatches with Charles. His conversion at the end of the play is in pure fairy-tale tradition, but since he is left in Celia's hands the reformation will probably be a lasting one.

How so genial a fellow as Touchstone manages to steer a safe course in this super-charged atmosphere is a matter for interesting speculation. From the Duke he would never get more than a wry smile, Le Beau would try to cap his wit, and Rosalind would do it without trying! No wonder he blossoms in the jolly company of Corin, a perfect sharer of his dry, sly humor; and he relaxes to the point of matrimony with Audrey, that uninhibited rag-bag of giggles and monosyllables.

Once in the Forest, with what ease the Warwickshire of his youth takes hold of the playwright. These people he knows; with their country arguments and slow good humor, he is at home. Their kindliness is contrasted with the roguery of Oliver Martext, the hedgepriest whom scholars identify with one Marprelate, a Puritan preacher: "his name in everyone's mouth, his pamphlets in everyone's hands." But this fellow wrote no pamphlets. He is a rogue and Jaques who knows him, warns Touchstone: "Get you to church, and have a good priest that can tell you what marriage is; this fellow will but join you together as they join wainscot; then one of you will prove a shrunk panel and like green timber, warp, warp." Then why is he *Sir* Oliver Martext? Surely the title is stolen, like his clothes; dressed as he is from the scarecrows in the farmers' fields, with hat or cloak or shawl snatched from the hook by a farmhouse door on his quick exit after a free meal.

Poor, guileless Will'um, with whom Audrey was quite content till Touchstone took her giggling fancy, can be found in any of half a dozen hamlets to this day. Phebe the spoiled village beauty, with dreams above her station, and Silvius the lovelorn shepherd turned poet for a while by love—all these are as real as the brown forest paths they tread and must surely be played for the true fun that is in their natures, not for clowning.

Deep in the forest is the Banished Duke, more than half hunting squire, reveling in the outdoor life and the company of true friends and foresters, with a quiet poetry in his nature and a love of music so typical of his kind. Fortunate in Amiens and Foresters who sing, and pages who carol prettily. We used the Arne and traditional settings for the songs, not for fear of adventure but because they are so exquisitely true to the spirit of the play. Of this group of characters the most interesting is of course the Melancholy Jaques. In Watteau costume he looked like Jean Jacques Rousseau, wandering the forest with a book. He is the one person in the play who meets all the other groups before the end of the play. Men call to him more strongly in adversity than at ease, perhaps because he is looking always for the true man. He is the eternal questioner.

Then there is the final group, who to most people are the play—Rosalind, Celia and Orlando. I suppose every English-speaking actress has longed to play Rosalind, many without realizing until too late that she talks too much! "Do you not know I am a woman? When I think, I must speak." Only an actress of infinite resource, variety and wit can do justice to the part. Her scenes with Orlando are not just a battle of words. Besides her wit and gaiety there are her moments of fear and bewilderment at her banishment, of tenderness in love, of anger with Phebe and of real apprehension in the bloody napkin scene. She is a very rainbow of a woman, glittering and sparkling through the summer showers.

Orlando is not very easy. He is not merely a romantic lover, carving Rosalind on forest trees. He has the capacity for infinite amusement with the young "Ganymede"; how gaily he caps his sallies and leads "him" on to fresh and outrageous fun. Add to this the young gallant who dared a match with the redoubtable court wrestler, and then, himself exhausted, carried a failing Adam into the Duke's stronghold at the sword's point, and later rescued his ill-intentioned brother from a lioness and a snake, and you have quite a person!

Last, but by no means least, there is Celia, a most delightful character. It is obvious from the first that she is fearless, loyal and loving; but she is more. The adventure into Arden is her idea, she plans it, all the practical work is hers. But she is no mere Martha; she takes and gives her share of fun, which is all pure gain to the play. The problem is that she is present throughout most of the love scenes, forgotten for long stretches by the lovers, though not by the audience. We put her in a Watteau swing, hung from the trees, for part of the time, and at one point the lovers played across her while they swung her, and then forgot her! Shakespeare never lets us see her in love; she might steal the play if he did; or perhaps he was ashamed of himself for fobbing her off with Oliver!

The bulk of the play is prose of great beauty, interspersed with punning doggerel and of course much blank verse.

There is one moment when the language becomes a spoken madrigal for four voices: Phebe, Silvius, Rosalind and Orlando. I mean the passage which Phebe starts with the line:

Good shepherd, tell this youth what 'tis to love.

This passage, taken with the cadence and speed of music, has an infectious beauty that captivates an audience. The Masque of Hymen at the end of the play can also have a rustic prettiness. Who could the girls dress up as Hymen but one of the Duke's singing pages, with the Foresters to carry him in in a litter of boughs? We set the play in the early fall, and Hymen scattered autumn leaves as he sang.

There are questions. Why do Orlando and Oliver not recognize Celia? Does Oliver recognize her? Does he tell Orlando and has Orlando guessed who Ganymede really is at the point when he exclaims: "Oh, how bitter a thing it is to look into happiness through another man's eyes!"? Does Jaques recognize Rosalind in the "Traveler" scene? Why does he not recognize Touchstone, or does he but keeps his counsel? How much does Touchstone let out to Corin, that they talk so freely of the Court? The answer to these must be "As you like it."

The play must be played at a good allover speed and though the country folk are slower, they must never pull it down to less than a jog trot. This means that seconds only can be allowed for scene changes. We framed the whole Forest, which was set throughout, in two great trees, downstage. Behind these we dropped a framed half cloth of a high orchard wall, with espaliered fruit trees upon it, and a practical door into the inner garden set in it, for the scenes in Oliver's orchard. The set for Duke Frederick's court was a semicircular balustrade on casters, with a statue of Cupid, which was garlanded with flowers during the opening dialogue between Rosalind and Celia. The balustrade formed an arena for the wrestling, cutting off the onlookers. The background for both these settings was the shadowy depth of trees, never fully lit until the Forest of Arden was revealed. The main scene was backed by gauzes which enabled the lighting to create great variety of time and place. In the scenes near Celia's cottage, we had free-standing ground rows of split chestnut fence and corn stooks. Trunks of many heights and sizes were used for the part of the forest by the Duke's cave. These were like the sandstone rocks out of which in Warwickshire the great oaks and beeches grow. This device enabled Amiens to sing "Blow, blow, thou winter wind," leaning against one of the large downstage trees in a shaft of moonlight, while the Duke talked with Orlando and the rest listened to the song, in the flickering glow of the campfire, over which, in the sunset, we had watched them cook their evening meal. Here I would like to pay grateful tribute to that fine artist in the theatre, Molly McArthur, who was responsible for the scenery and costumes.

I have throughout this commentary on the production said *we* because, although I directed the play, what is the director without the actors? In a play so familiar as this one is, the actors will have many ideas which the director is there to blend into a whole; he may not only exploit his own fancy. Never was director more fortunate. What a cast it was! William Devlin, Duke Frederick; Ernest Hare, the Banished Duke; Milton Rosmer, Touchstone. James Dale and later Leon Quartermaine played Jaques; Freda Jackson, Audrey. Eileen Peel and later Marie Ney played Celia. Young Michael Redgrave, playing his first season at the Old Vic, was Orlando and the incomparable Edith Evans, Rosalind. And believe it or not, there was Alec Guinness giving a foretaste of his astonishing versatility, doubling the tiny parts of Le Beau and Jaques de Boys!

As the autumn sun set on the last scene and Rosalind stepped forward to speak the epilogue, it was nice to think of them all going home in love and friendliness, to great log fires and warm beds for the winter:

> When icicles hang by the wall,
> And Dick the shepherd blows his nail,
> When Tom brings logs into the hall,
> And milk comes frozen home in pail. . . .

But that's the ending of another play!

As You Like It

DRAMATIS PERSONAE — *players*

DUKE SENIOR.

DUKE FREDERICK, *his brother, usurper of his dukedom.*

AMIENS,
JAQUES, } *lords attending on Duke Senior.*

LE BEAU, *a courtier attending on Duke Frederick.*

CHARLES, *wrestler to Duke Frederick.*

OLIVER,
JAQUES, } *sons of Sir Rowland de Boys.*
ORLANDO,

ADAM,
DENNIS, } *servants to Oliver.*

TOUCHSTONE, *a clown.*

SIR OLIVER MARTEX, *a vicar.*

CORIN,
SILVIUS, } *shepherds.*

WILLIAM, *a country fellow.*

HYMEN. — *god of marriage*

ROSALIND, *daughter to Duke Senior.*

CELIA, *daughter to Duke Frederick.*

PHEBE, *a shepherdess.*

AUDREY, *a country girl.*

LORDS, PAGES, *and* ATTENDANTS, *&c.*

SCENE—*Oliver's house; Duke Frederick's court; and the Forest of Arden.*

Act one Scene one

*Orchard of Oliver's house. Enter
Orlando and Adam.*

ORLANDO

As I remember, Adam, it was upon this fashion
bequeathed me by will but poor a thousand
crowns, and, as thou sayst, charged my brother
on his blessing to breed me well; and there begins
my sadness. My brother Jaques he keeps at   5
school, and report speaks goldenly of his profit;
for my part, hè keeps me rustically at home, or,
to speak more properly, stays me here at home
unkept; for call you that keeping for a gentleman
of my birth, that differs not from the stalling of   10
an ox? His horses are bred better; for besides
that they are fair with their feeding they are
taught their manage, and to that end riders
dearly hired; but I, his brother, gain nothing under him but growth, for the which his animals on 15
his dunghills are as much bound to him as I. Besides this nothing that he so plentifully gives me,
the something that nature gave me, his countenance seems to take from me; he lets me feed
with his hinds, bars me the place of a brother,   20
and as much as in him lies mines my gentility

A complete Glossary of Elizabethan terms begins
on page 184.

with my education. This is it Adam, that grieves
me; and the spirit of my father, which I think is
within me, begins to mutiny against this servi-
tude. I will no longer endure it, though yet I   25
know no wise remedy how to avoid it.

Enter Oliver. — mistreated orlando

ADAM

Yonder comes my master, your brother.

ORLANDO'

Go apart Adam, and thou shalt hear how he will
shake me up. stand and listen   30
                            withdraws

OLIVER

Now sir, what make you here?

ORLANDO

Nothing. I am not taught to make anything.

OLIVER

What mar you then sir?

ORLANDO

Marry sir, I am helping you to mar that which   35
God made, a poor unworthy brother of yours,
with idleness.

OLIVER

Marry sir, be better employed, and be naught
awhile.

ORLANDO

Shall I keep your hogs, and eat husks with them?   40
What prodigal portion have I spent, that I should
come to such penury? (want)

OLIVER

Know you where you are sir?

mar – by the virgin mary

ORLANDO

O sir, very well. Here in your orchard.

OLIVER

Know you before whom sir? 45

ORLANDO

Ay, better than him I am before knows me. I know you are my eldest brother, and in the gentle condition of blood you should so know me. The courtesy of nations allows you my better, in that you are the first born, but the same tradition 50 takes not away my blood, were there twenty brothers betwixt us. I have as much of my father in me as you, albeit I confess your coming before me is nearer to his reverence.

OLIVER

What, boy!   [*Strikes him.* 55

ORLANDO

Come come, elder brother, you are too young in this.   [*Holds him.*

OLIVER

Wilt thou lay hands on me villain?

ORLANDO

I am no villain; I am the youngest son of Sir Rowland de Boys; he was my father, and he is 60 thrice a villain that says such a father begot villains. Wert thou not my brother, I would not take this hand from thy throat till this other had pulled out thy tongue for saying so. Thou hast railed on thyself. 65

Charles - professional Wrestler

ADAM

Sweet masters be patient. For your father's remembrance, be at accord.

OLIVER

Let me go I say.

treat me right or let me go

ORLANDO

I will not till I please. You shall hear me. My father charged you in his will to give me good   70
education. You have trained me like a peasant, obscuring and hiding from me all gentleman-like qualities. The spirit of my father grows strong in me, and I will no longer endure it. Therefore allow me such exercises as may become a gentle-   75
man, or give me the poor allottery my father left me by testament; with that I will go buy my fortunes.

OLIVER

And what wilt thou do? Beg when that is spent? Well sir, get you in. I will not long be troubled   80
with you. You shall have some part of your will. I pray you leave me.

ORLANDO

I will no further offend you than becomes me for my good.

OLIVER   *says to Adam.*

Get you with him, you old dog.   85

ADAM

Is old dog my reward? Most true, I have lost my teeth in your service. God be with my old master, he would not have spoke such a word.

> [*Exeunt Orlando and Adam.*

OLIVER

Is it even so; begin you to grow upon me? I will 90
physic your rankness, and yet give no thousand
crowns neither. Holla Dennis!

> *Enter Dennis.*

DENNIS

Calls your worship?

OLIVER

Was not Charles the Duke's wrestler here to
speak with me? 95

DENNIS

So please you, he is here at the door, and impor-
tunes access to you.

OLIVER

Call him in.   [*Dennis goes to the door.*
'Twill be a good way; and to-morrow the
wrestling is.

> *Enter Charles.*

CHARLES

Good morrow to your worship.   [*Exit Dennis.* 100

OLIVER

Good Monsieur Charles. What's the new news at
the new court?

CHARLES

There's no news at the court sir, but the old
news. That is, the old Duke is banished by his
younger brother the new Duke; and three or four 105
loving lords have put themselves into voluntary

exile with him, whose lands and revenues enrich
the new Duke; therefore he gives them good
leave to wander.

OLIVER

Can you tell if Rosalind the Duke's daughter be   110
banished with her father?

CHARLES

O no; for the Duke's daughter her cousin so loves
her, being ever from their cradles bred together,
that she would have followed her exile, or have
died to stay behind her. She is at the court, and   115
no less beloved of her uncle than his own daughter, and never two ladies loved as they do.

OLIVER

Where will the old Duke live?

CHARLES

They say he is already in the forest of Arden, and   120
a many merry men with him; and there they live
like the old Robin Hood of England. They say
many young gentlemen flock to him every day,
and fleet the time carelessly as they did in the
golden world.   125

OLIVER

What, you wrestle to-morrow before the new
Duke?

CHARLES

Marry do I sir; and I came to acquaint you with
a matter. I am given sir, secretly to understand
that your younger brother Orlando hath a dis-   130
position to come in disguised against me to try a

fall. To-morrow sir, I wrestle for my credit, and
he that escapes me without some broken limb
shall acquit him well. Your brother is but young
and tender, and for your love I would be loth to 135
foil him, as I must for my own honour if he
come in. Therefore out of my love to you, I came
hither to acquaint you withal, that either you
might stay him from his intendment, or brook
such disgrace well as he shall run into, in that 140
it is a thing of his own search, and altogether
against my will.

OLIVER

Charles, I thank thee for thy love to me, which
thou shalt find I will most kindly requite. I had
myself notice of my brother's purpose herein, 145
and have by underhand means laboured to dissuade him from it; but he is resolute. I'll tell thee
Charles, it is the stubbornest young fellow of
France, full of ambition, an envious emulator of
every man's good parts, a secret and villainous 150
contriver against me his natural brother. Therefore use thy discretion; I had as lief thou didst
break his neck as his finger. And thou wert best
look to't; for if thou dost him any slight disgrace,
or if he do not mightily grace himself on thee, he 155
will practise against thee by poison, entrap thee
by some treacherous device, and never leave thee
till he hath ta'en thy life by some indirect means
or other; for I assure thee, and almost with tears
I speak it, there is not one so young and so vil- 160

lainous this day living. I speak but brotherly of
him, but should I anatomize him to thee as he
is, I must blush, and weep, and thou must look
pale and wonder.   *I'm his brother*

CHARLES   *or I could say more*

I am heartily glad I came hither to you. If he 165
come to-morrow, I'll give him his payment. If
ever he go alone again, I'll never wrestle for prize
more. And so God keep your worship.

OLIVER

Farewell good Charles. [*Exit Charles.*] Now will
I stir this gamester. I hope I shall see an end of 170
him; for my soul, yet I know not why, hates
nothing more than he. Yet he's gentle, never
schooled, and yet learned, full of noble device, of
all sorts enchantingly beloved, and indeed so
much in the heart of the world, and especially of 175
my own people, who best know him, that I am
altogether misprised. But it shall not be so long;
this wrestler shall clear all. Nothing remains but
that I kindle the boy thither; which now I'll go
about.   [*Exit.* 180

Scene two

> *Lawn before the Duke's palace. Enter
> Rosalind and Celia.*

CELIA

I pray thee Rosalind, sweet my coz, be merry.

ROSALIND

Dear Celia, I show more mirth than I am mistress of, and would you yet I were merrier? Unless you could teach me to forget a banished   5
father, you must not learn me how to remember
any extraordinary pleasure.

CELIA

Herein I see thou lov'st me not with the full
weight that I love thee. If my uncle thy banished
father had banished thy uncle the Duke my fa-   10
ther, so thou hadst been still with me, I could
have taught my love to take thy father for mine.
So wouldst thou, if the truth of thy love to me
were so righteously tempered, as mine is to thee.   15

ROSALIND

Well, I will forget the condition of my estate, to
rejoice in yours.

CELIA

You know my father hath no child but I, nor
none is like to have: and truly when he dies, thou
shalt be his heir; for what he hath taken away   20
from thy father perforce, I will render thee again
in affection; by mine honour I will; and when I
break that oath, let me turn monster. Therefore
my sweet Rose, my dear Rose, be merry.   25

ROSALIND

From henceforth I will coz, and devise sports.
Let me see, what think you of falling in love?

CELIA

Marry I prithee do, to make sport withal. But

love no man in good earnest, nor no further in 30
sport neither than with safety of a pure blush
thou mayst in honour come off again.

ROSALIND

What shall be our sport then?

CELIA

Let us sit and mock the good housewife Fortune
from her wheel, that her gifts may henceforth be 35
bestowed equally.

ROSALIND

I would we could do so; for her benefits are
mightily misplaced, and the bountiful blind
woman doth most mistake in her gifts to women.

CELIA

'Tis true, for those that she makes fair, she scarce 40
makes honest, and those that she makes honest,
she makes very ill-favouredly. *chaste —*
pure moral

ROSALIND

Nay, now thou goest from Fortune's office to Nature's. Fortune reigns in gifts of the world, not
in the lineaments of Nature. 45

Enter Touchstone.

CELIA

No? When Nature hath made a fair creature,
may she not by Fortune fall into the fire? Though
Nature hath given us wit to flout at Fortune, hath
not Fortune sent in this fool to cut off the argument? 50

ROSALIND

Indeed, there is Fortune too hard for Nature,

when Fortune makes Nature's natural the cutter-
off of Nature's wit.

CELIA

Peradventure this is not Fortune's work neither,
but Nature's, who perceiveth our natural wits too   55
dull to reason of such goddesses and hath sent
this natural for our whetstone; for always the
dulness of the fool is the whetstone of the wits.
How now wit, whither wander you?

TOUCHSTONE

Mistress, you must come away to your father.   60

CELIA

Were you made the messenger?

TOUCHSTONE

No by mine honour, but I was bid to come for
you.

ROSALIND

Where learned you that oath fool?   65

TOUCHSTONE

Of a certain knight, that swore by his honour
they were good pancakes, and swore by his honour the mustard was naught. Now I'll stand to it,
the pancakes were naught, and the mustard was
good, and yet was not the knight forsworn.   70

CELIA

How prove you that in the great heap of your
knowledge?

ROSALIND

Ay marry, now unmuzzle your wisdom.

TOUCHSTONE

Stand you both forth now. Stroke your chins, 75
and swear by your beards that I am a knave.

CELIA

By our beards, if we had them, thou art.

TOUCHSTONE

By my knavery, if I had it, then I were. But if 80
you swear by that that is not, you are not forsworn. No more was this knight, swearing by his
honour, for he never had any; or if he had, he
had sworn it away, before ever he saw those pancakes, or that mustard.   85

CELIA

Prithee, who is't that thou mean'st?

TOUCHSTONE

One that old Frederick your father loves.

CELIA

My father's love is enough to honour him.
Enough, speak no more of him. You'll be   90
whipped for taxation one of these days.

TOUCHSTONE

The more pity that fools may not speak wisely
what wise men do foolishly.

CELIA

By my troth thou sayest true; for since the little
wit that fools have was silenced, the little foolery 95
that wise men have makes a great show.

Enter Le Beau

Here comes Monsieur Le Beau.

ROSALIND

With his mouth full of news.

CELIA

Which he will put on us, as pigeons feed their
young. 100

ROSALIND

Then shall we be news-crammed.

CELIA

All the better. We shall be the more marketable.
Bon jour Monsieur Le Beau, what's the news?

LE BEAU

Fair Princess, you have lost much good sport. 105

CELIA

Sport? Of what colour?

LE BEAU

What colour madam? How shall I answer you?

ROSALIND

As wit and fortune will. 110

TOUCHSTONE

Or as the Destinies decrees.

CELIA

Well said, that was laid on with a trowel.

TOUCHSTONE

Nay, if I keep not my rank—

ROSALIND

Thou losest thy old smell.

LE BEAU

You amaze me ladies. I would have told you of 115
good wrestling, which you have lost the sight of.

ROSALIND

Yet tell us the manner of the wrestling.

LE BEAU

I will tell you the beginning; and if it please your
ladyships you may see the end, for the best is yet   120
to do, and here where you are they are coming
to perform it.

CELIA

Well, the beginning that is dead and buried.

LE BEAU

There comes an old man, and his three sons—   125

CELIA

I could match this beginning with an old tale.

LE BEAU

Three proper young men, of excellent growth
and presence—   130

ROSALIND

With bills on their necks: be it known unto all
men by these presents.

LE BEAU

The eldest of the three wrestled with Charles the
Duke's wrestler, which Charles in a moment
threw him, and broke three of his ribs, that there   135
is little hope of life in him. So he served the second, and so the third. Yonder they lie, the poor
old man their father making such pitiful dole
over them, that all the beholders take his part
with weeping. *pity orlando —*   140

ROSALIND

Alas!

TOUCHSTONE

But what is the sport monsieur, that the ladies have lost?

LE BEAU

Why this that I speak of.

TOUCHSTONE

Thus men may grow wiser every day. It is the 145 first time that ever I heard breaking of ribs was sport for ladies.

CELIA

Or I, I promise thee.

ROSALIND

But is there any else longs to see this broken music in his sides? Is there yet another dotes 150 upon rib-breaking? Shall we see this wrestling cousin?

LE BEAU

You must if you stay here, for here is the place appointed for the wrestling, and they are ready to perform it. 155

CELIA

Yonder sure they are coming: let us now stay and see it.

Flourish. Enter Duke Frederick, Lords, Orlando, Charles, and Attendants.

DUKE FREDERICK — *father of Celia*

Come on. Since the youth will not be entreated, his own peril on his forwardness. *yes —*

ROSALIND

Is yonder the man? 160

LE BEAU

Even he, madam.

CELIA

Alas, he is too young. Yet he looks successfully.

DUKE FREDERICK

How now daughter, and cousin, are you crept
hither to see the wrestling?   165

ROSALIND

Ay my liege, so please you give us leave.

DUKE FREDERICK

You will take little delight in it, I can tell you,
there is such odds in the man. In pity of the
challenger's youth, I would fain dissuade him,   170
but he will not be entreated. Speak to him ladies;
see if you can move him.   *try to keep him from fight.*

CELIA

Call him hither, good Monsieur Le Beau.

DUKE FREDERICK

Do so: I'll not be by.

LE BEAU

Monsieur the challenger, the Princess calls for   175
you.

ORLANDO

I attend them with all respect and duty.

ROSALIND

Young man, have you challenged Charles the
wrestler?

ORLANDO

No fair Princess. He is the general challenger: I   18

Purpose of Le Beau

come but in as others do to try with him the
strength of my youth.

CELIA

Young gentleman, your spirits are too bold for
your years. You have seen cruel proof of this
man's strength. If you saw yourself with your   185
eyes, or knew yourself with your judgement, the
fear of your adventure would counsel you to a
more equal enterprise. We pray you for your own
sake to embrace your own safety, and give over
this attempt.   190

ROSALIND

Do young sir; your reputation shall not therefore be misprised. We will make it our suit to the
Duke that the wrestling might not go forward.

ORLANDO   *polite*

I beseech you, punish me not with your hard   195
thoughts, wherein I confess me much guilty to
deny so fair and excellent ladies any thing. But
let your fair eyes and gentle wishes go with me
to my trial; wherein if I be foiled, there is but one
shamed that was never gracious; if killed, but   200
one dead that is willing to be so. I shall do my
friends no wrong, for I have none to lament me;
the world no injury, for in it I have nothing;
only in the world I fill up a place, which may be
better supplied when I have made it empty.   205

ROSALIND

The little strength that I have, I would it were
with you.

Oliver

CELIA

And mine, to eke out hers.

ROSALIND

Fare you well. Pray heaven I be deceived in you.   210

CELIA

Your heart's desires be with you.

CHARLES

Come, where is this young gallant, that is so desirous to lie with his mother earth?

ORLANDO

Ready sir; but his will hath in it a more modest
working.   215

DUKE FREDERICK

You shall try but one fall.

CHARLES

No, I warrant your Grace, you shall not entreat
him to a second, that have so mightily persuaded
him from a first.

ORLANDO

You mean to mock me after. You should not   220
have mocked me before. But come your ways.

ROSALIND

Now Hercules be thy speed, young man.

CELIA

I would I were invisible, to catch the strong
fellow by the leg.   [*They wrestle.*

ROSALIND

O excellent young man.   225

CELIA

If I had a thunderbolt in mine eye, I can tell who

should down.   [*Shout. Charles is thrown.*

DUKE FREDERICK
No more, no more.

ORLANDO
Yes I beseech your Grace, I am not yet well
breathed.   230

DUKE FREDERICK
How dost thou Charles?

LE BEAU
He cannot speak my lord.

DUKE FREDERICK
Bear him away. [*Attendants carry Charles out.*]
What is thy name, young man?

ORLANDO
Orlando my liege, the youngest son of Sir Row- 235
land de Boys.

DUKE FREDERICK
I would thou hadst been son to some man else.
The world esteemed thy father honourable,
But I did find him still mine enemy.
Thou shouldst have better pleased me with this
    deed,
                                                            240
Hadst thou descended from another house.
But fare thee well, thou art a gallant youth;
I would thou hadst told me of another father.
                            [*Exeunt Duke Frederick,
                                Le Beau, and Lords.*

CELIA
Were I my father, coz, would I do this?

ORLANDO *loves father*

I am more proud to be Sir Rowland's son,
His youngest son, and would not change that
    calling   245
To be adopted heir to Frederick.

ROSALIND *cried so he wouldn't fight.*

My father loved Sir Rowland as his soul,
And all the world was of my father's mind.
Had I before known this young man his son
I should have given him tears unto entreaties,   250
Ere he should thus have ventured.

CELIA
                              Gentle cousin,
Let us go thank him, and encourage him.
My father's rough and envious disposition
Sticks me at heart. Sir, you have well deserved.
If you do keep your promises in love   255
But justly, as you have exceeded all promise,
Your mistress shall be happy.

ROSALIND
                              Gentleman,
          [*Gives him a chain from her neck.*
Wear this for me, one out of suits with fortune,
That would give more, but that her hand lacks
    means.
Shall we go coz?

CELIA
                    Ay. Fare you well, fair gentleman.   260

ORLANDO
Can I not say, I thank you? My better parts

Are all thrown down, and that which here stands
   up
Is but a quintain, a mere lifeless block.

    ROSALIND

He calls us back. My pride fell with my fortunes;
I'll ask him what he would. Did you call, sir?   265
Sir, you have wrestled well, and overthrown
More than your enemies.

    CELIA

              Will you go coz?

    ROSALIND

Have with you. Fare you well.

      [*Exeunt Rosalind and Celia.*

    ORLANDO

What passion hangs these weights upon my
   tongue?
I cannot speak to her, yet she urged conference.   270
    Enter Le Beau.
O poor Orlando, thou art overthrown.
Or Charles, or something weaker, masters thee.

    LE BEAU

Good sir, I do in friendship counsel you
To leave this place. Albeit you have deserved
High commendation, true applause, and love,   275
Yet such is now the Duke's condition
That he misconsters all that you have done.
The Duke is humorous: what he is indeed
More suits you to conceive than I to speak of.

    ORLANDO

I thank you sir; and pray you tell me this,   280

Which of the two was daughter of the Duke,
That here was at the wrestling?

    LE BEAU

Neither his daughter, if we judge by manners;
But yet indeed the smaller [1] is his daughter:
The other is daughter to the banished Duke,   285
And here detained by her usurping uncle,
To keep his daughter company; whose loves
Are dearer than the natural bond of sisters.
But I can tell you that of late this Duke
Hath ta'en displeasure 'gainst his gentle niece,   290
Grounded upon no other argument
But that the people praise her for her virtues,
And pity her, for her good father's sake;
And on my life his malice 'gainst the lady
Will suddenly break forth. Sir, fare you well.   295
Hereafter, in a better world than this,
I shall desire more love and knowledge of you.

        ORLANDO

I rest much bounden to you; fare you well.

                              [*Exit Le Beau.*

Thus must I from the smoke into the smother,
From tyrant Duke unto a tyrant brother.   300
But heavenly Rosalind!   [*Exit.*

---

[1] *Taller* (F.1.)

Scene three

*A room in the palace. Enter Celia and
Rosalind.*

CELIA

Why cousin, why Rosalind; Cupid have mercy,
not a word?

ROSALIND

Not one to throw at a dog.

CELIA

No, thy words are too precious to be cast away
upon curs; throw some of them at me; come lame   5
me with reasons.

ROSALIND

Then there were two cousins laid up, when the
one should be lamed with reasons, and the other
mad without any.

CELIA

But is all this for your father?   10

ROSALIND

No, some of it is for my child's father. O how
full of briers is this working-day world!

CELIA

They are but burs, cousin, thrown upon thee in
holiday foolery; if we walk not in the trodden
paths our very petticoats will catch them.   15

ROSALIND

I could shake them off my coat; these burs are in
my heart.

CELIA

Hem them away.

ROSALIND

I would try, if I could cry hem, and have him.   20

CELIA

Come, come, wrestle with thy affections.

ROSALIND

O they take the part of a better wrestler than myself.

CELIA

O, a good wish upon you; you will cry in time
in despite of a fall. But turning these jests out of   25
service let us talk in good earnest. Is it possible,
on such a sudden, you should fall into so strong a
liking with old Sir Rowland's youngest son?

ROSALIND

The Duke my father loved his father dearly.   30

CELIA

Doth it therefore ensue that you should love his
son dearly? By this kind of chase, I should hate
him, for my father hated his father dearly; yet I
hate not Orlando.   *doesnt hate just*   35
                     because his father
ROSALIND   *does.*

No faith, hate him not, for my sake.

CELIA

Why should I not? Doth he not deserve well?

ROSALIND

Let me love him for that, and do you love him
because I do.

Enter Duke Frederick, with Lords.

Look here comes the Duke. 40
>   CELIA

With his eyes full of anger.
>   DUKE FREDERICK

Mistress, dispatch you with your safest haste,
And get you from our court.
>   ROSALIND

>   Me uncle?
>   DUKE FREDERICK

>   You cousin.

Within these ten days if that thou beest found 45
So near our public court as twenty miles,
Thou diest for it.
>   ROSALIND

>   I do beseech your Grace,

Let me the knowledge of my fault bear with me.
If with myself I hold intelligence,
Or have acquaintance with mine own desires; 50
If that I do not dream, or be not frantic—
As I do trust I am not—then dear uncle,
Never so much as in a thought unborn
Did I offend your Highness.
>   DUKE FREDERICK

>   Thus do all traitors.

If their purgation did consist in words, 55
They are as innocent as grace itself.
Let it suffice thee that I trust thee not.
>   ROSALIND

Yet your mistrust cannot make me a traitor.
Tell me whereon the likelihood depends.

DUKE FREDERICK

Thou art thy father's daughter, there's enough.   60

ROSALIND

So was I when your Highness took his dukedom;
So was I when your Highness banished him.
Treason is not inherited, my lord,
Or if we did derive it from our friends,
What's that to me, my father was no traitor.   65
Then good my liege mistake me not so much
To think my poverty is treacherous.

CELIA

Dear sovereign hear me speak.

DUKE FREDERICK

Ay Celia, we stayed her for your sake,
Else had she with her father ranged along.   70

CELIA

I did not then entreat to have her stay;
It was your pleasure, and your own remorse.
I was too young that time to value her,
But now I know her. If she be a traitor,
Why so am I; we still have slept together,   75
Rose at an instant, learned, played, eat together;
And wheresoe'er we went, like Juno's swans,
Still we went coupled and inseparable.

DUKE FREDERICK

She is too subtle for thee; and her smoothness,
Her very silence and her patience,   80
Speak to the people, and they pity her.
Thou art a fool; she robs thee of thy name,

And thou wilt show more bright and seem more
    virtuous
When she is gone. Then open not thy lips.
Firm and irrevocable is my doom   85
Which I have passed upon her; she is banished.

CELIA

Pronounce that sentence then on me, my liege.
I cannot live out of her company.

DUKE FREDERICK

You are a fool. You, niece, provide yourself.
If you outstay the time, upon mine honour,   90
And in the greatness of my word, you die.

    [*Exeunt Duke Frederick and Lords.*

CELIA

O my poor Rosalind, whither wilt thou go?
Wilt thou change fathers? I will give thee mine.
I charge thee be not thou more grieved than I am.

ROSALIND

I have more cause.

CELIA

                    Thou hast not cousin.   95
Prithee be cheerful; know'st thou not the Duke
Hath banished me his daughter?

ROSALIND

                    That he hath not.

CELIA

No, hath not? Rosalind lacks then the love
Which teacheth me that thou and I am one.
Shall we be sundered? Shall we part, sweet girl?   100
No, let my father seek another heir.

Therefore devise with me how we may fly,
Whither to go, and what to bear with us;
And do not seek to take your change upon you,
To bear your griefs yourself, and leave me out.   105
For by this heaven, now at our sorrows pale,
Say what thou canst, I'll go along with thee.

    ROSALIND
Why, whither shall we go?

    CELIA
To seek my uncle in the forest of Arden.

    ROSALIND
Alas, what danger will it be to us,   110
Maids as we are, to travel forth so far.
Beauty provoketh thieves sooner than gold.

    CELIA
I'll put myself in poor and mean attire,
And with a kind of umber smirch my face.
The like do you, so shall we pass along   115
And never stir assailants.

    ROSALIND
                    Were it not better,
Because that I am more than common tall,
That I did suit me all points like a man?
A gallant curtle-axe upon my thigh,
A boar-spear in my hand, and in my heart   120
Lie there what hidden woman's fear there will,
We'll have a swashing and a martial outside,
As many other mannish cowards have
That do outface it with their semblances.

Ganymede on Eagle - stolen -
traded for horses.

CELIA

What shall I call thee when thou art a man? 125

ROSALIND

I'll have no worse a name than Jove's own page,
And therefore look you call me Ganymede. *- traded*
for horses.
But what will you be called?

CELIA

Something that hath a reference to my state.
No longer Celia, but Aliena. 130
tried

ROSALIND

But cousin, what if we assayed to steal
The clownish fool out of your father's court?
Would he not be a comfort to our travel?

CELIA

He'll go along o'er the wide world with me;
Leave me alone to woo him. Let's away 135
And get our jewels and our wealth together;
Devise the fittest time and safest way
To hide us from pursuit that will be made
After my flight. Now go in we content
To liberty, and not to banishment.   [*Exeunt.* 140

Act two Scene one

The Forest of Arden. Enter Duke Senior,
Amiens, and two or three Lords. *father of*
Rosalind

DUKE SENIOR

Now my co-mates and brothers in exile,
Hath not old custom made this life more sweet

Than that of painted pomp? Are not these woods
More free from peril than the envious court?
Here feel we not the penalty of Adam,   **5**
The seasons' difference, as the icy fang
And churlish chiding of the winter's wind,
Which when it bites and blows upon my body
Even till I shrink with cold, I smile, and say   *not like a*
This is no flattery; these are counsellors   *person* **10**
That feelingly persuade me what I am.
Sweet are the uses of adversity,
Which, like the toad ugly and venomous,   *poisonous*
Wears yet a precious jewel in his head.   *eye*
And this our life, exempt from public haunt,   *life at* **15**
Finds tongues in trees, books in the running   *Castle*
    brooks,
Sermons in stones, and good in every thing.

     AMIENS

I would not change it. Happy is your Grace,
That can translate the stubbornness of fortune
Into so quiet and so sweet a style.   **20**

     DUKE SENIOR

Come, shall we go and kill us venison?
And yet it irks me the poor dappled fools,
Being native burghers of this desert city,
Should in their own confines with forked heads
Have their round haunches gored.

     FIRST LORD

               Indeed my lord   **25**
The melancholy Jaques grieves at that,
And in that kind swears you do more usurp

alliteration

blank Verse

Than doth your brother that hath banished you,
To-day my Lord of Amiens and myself
Did steal behind him as he lay along
Under an oak, whose antique root peeps out   30
Upon the brook that brawls along this wood,
To the which place a poor sequestered stag,
That from the hunter's aim had ta'en a hurt,
Did come to languish; and indeed my lord,   35
The wretched animal heaved forth such groans
That their discharge did stretch his leathern coat
Almost to bursting, and the big round tears
Coursed one another down his innocent nose
In piteous chase; and thus the hairy fool,   40
Much marked of the melancholy Jaques,
Stood on th' extremest verge of the swift brook,
Augmenting it with tears.

DUKE SENIOR

But what said Jaques?
Did he not moralise this spectacle?

FIRST LORD

O yes, into a thousand similes.   45
First, for his weeping into the needless stream,
Poor deer, quoth he, thou mak'st a testament
As worldings do, giving thy sum of more
To that which had too much. Then being there
     alone,
Left and abandoned of his velvet friend.   50
'Tis right, quoth he, thus misery doth part
The flux of company. Anon a careless herd,
Full of the pasture, jumps along by him,

And never stays to greet him. Ay, quoth Jaques,
Sweep on you fat and greasy citizens,   55
'Tis just the fashion; wherefore do you look
Upon that poor and broken bankrupt there?
Thus most invectively he pierceth through
The body of the country, city, court,
Yea, and of this our life, swearing that we   60
Are mere usurpers, tyrants, and what's worse,
To fright the animals, and to kill them up
In their assigned and native dwelling-place.

    DUKE SENIOR

And did you leave him in this contemplation?

    SECOND LORD

We did my lord, weeping and commenting   65
Upon the sobbing deer.

    DUKE SENIOR

               Show me the place.
I love to cope him in these sullen fits,
For then he's full of matter.

    FIRST LORD

I'll bring you to him straight.   [*Exeunt.*

Jack moralized.

Scene two

    *A room in the palace. Enter Duke Fred-
    erick, with Lords.*

    DUKE FREDERICK   *Celia is gone*

Can it be possible that no man saw them?
It cannot be; some villains of my court

Are of consent and sufferance in this.

      FIRST LORD

I cannot hear of any that did see her.
The ladies her attendants of her chamber   5
Saw her a-bed, and in the morning early,
They found the bed untreasured of their mistress.

      SECOND LORD

My lord, the roynish clown, at whom so oft
Your Grace was wont to laugh, is also missing.
Hisperia, the Princess' gentlewoman,   10
Confesses that she secretly o'erheard
Your daughter and her cousin much commend
The parts and graces of the wrestler *Orlando*
That did but lately foil the sinewy Charles,
And she believes wherever they are gone   15
That youth is surely in their company.

      DUKE FREDERICK

Send to his brother, fetch that gallant hither;
If he be absent, bring his brother to me;
I'll make him find him. Do this suddenly;
And let not search and inquisition quail,   20
To bring again these foolish runaways. [*Exeunt.*

Scene three

    Before Oliver's house. Enter Orlando
    and Adam.

      ORLANDO
Who's there?

when people are successful, people are envious!

ADAM

What my young master? O my gentle master,
O my sweet master, o you memory
Of old Sir Rowland; why, what make you here?
Why are you virtuous? Why do people love you?   5
And wherefore are you gentle, strong, and
    valiant?   *(not anonyms)*
Why would you be so fond to overcome
The bony priser of the humorous Duke?
Your praise is come too swiftly home before you.
Know you not master, to some kind of men   10
Their graces serve them but as enemies?
No more do yours; your virtues, gentle master,
Are sanctified and holy traitors to you.
O what a world is this, when what is comely
Envenoms him that bears it.   15

ORLANDO

Why, what's the matter?

ADAM

                              O, unhappy youth,
Come not within these doors; within this roof
The enemy of all your graces lives.
Your brother, no, no brother, yet the son—
Yet not the son, I will not call him son—   20
Of him I was about to call his father,
Hath heard your praises, and this night he means
To burn the lodging where you use to lie,
And you within it; if he fail of that
He will have other means to cut you off.   25
I overheard him, and his practices.

Master of Characterization

This is no place, this house is but a butchery.
Abhor it, fear it, do not enter it.

ORLANDO

Why, whither Adam wouldst thou have me go?

ADAM

No matter whither, so you come not here. 30

ORLANDO

What, wouldst thou have me go and beg my
  food,
Or with a base and boisterous sword enforce *steel*
A thievish living on the common road?
This I must do, or know not what to do.
Yet this I will not do, do how I can; 35
I rather will subject me to the malice
Of a diverted blood and bloody brother.

ADAM

But do not so. I have five hundred crowns,
The thrifty hire I saved under your father,
Which I did store to be my foster-nurse 40
When service should in my old limbs lie lame,
And unregarded age in corners thrown.
Take that, and he that doth the ravens feed,
Yea providently caters for the sparrow,
Be comfort to my age. Here is the gold; 45
All this I give you. Let me be your servant.
Though I look old, yet I am strong and lusty.
For in my youth I never did apply
Hot and rebellious liquors in my blood,
Nor did not with unbashful forehead woo 50
The means of weakness and debility.

*debase —
make lower*

Therefore my age is as a lusty winter, *simile*
Frosty, but kindly. Let me go with you;
I'll do the service of a younger man
In all your business and necessities.   55

####### ORLANDO

O good old man, how well in thee appears
The constant service of the antique world,
When service sweat for duty, not for meed. *money*
Thou art not for the fashion of these times,
Where none will sweat, but for promotion,   60
And having that do choke their service up
Even with the having; it is not so with thee.
But poor old man, thou prun'st a rotten tree,
That cannot so much as a blossom yield
In lieu of all thy pains and husbandry.   65
But come thy ways, we'll go along together,
And ere we have thy youthful wages spent,
We'll light upon some settled low content.

####### ADAM

Master go on, and I will follow thee
To the last gasp with truth and loyalty.   70
From seventeen years, till now almost fourscore,
Here lived I, but now live here no more.
At seventeen years, many their fortunes seek,
But at fourscore it is too late a week.
Yet fortune cannot recompense me better   75
Than to die well, and not my master's debtor.
                                          [*Exeunt.*

(remuneration)
recompense

(Describing England) [handwritten]

Scene four *In France* [handwritten, struck through]

*The Forest of Arden. Enter Rosalind as
Ganymede, Celia as Aliena, and Touchstone.*

Zeus [handwritten]
ROSALIND

O Jupiter, how weary are my spirits.

TOUCHSTONE

I care not for my spirits, if my legs were not
weary.

ROSALIND

I could find in my heart to disgrace my man's apparel, and to cry like a woman; but I must com-   5
fort the weaker vessel, as doublet and hose ought
to show itself courageous to petticoat: therefore,
courage, good Aliena.

CELIA

double negative [handwritten]

I pray you bear with me. I cannot go no further.   10

TOUCHSTONE

For my part, I had rather bear with you than
bear you; yet I should bear no cross if I did bear
you, for I think you have no money in your
purse. *people with money have more
trials.* [handwritten]

ROSALIND

Well, this is the forest of Arden.   15

TOUCHSTONE

Ay, now am I in Arden, the more fool I; when I
was at home I was in a better place, but travel-
lers must be content.

ROSALIND

Ay, be so, good Touchstone.

Enter Corin and Silvius.

Look you, who comes here, a young man and an   20
old in solemn talk.

CORIN

That is the way to make her scorn you still.

SILVIUS

O Corin, that thou knew'st how I do love her.

CORIN

I partly guess; for I have loved ere now.

SILVIUS

No, Corin, being old, thou canst not guess,   25
Though in thy youth thou wast as true a lover
As ever sighed upon a midnight pillow.
But if thy love were ever like to mine,
As sure I think did never man love so,
How many actions most ridiculous   30
Hast thou been drawn to by thy fantasy?

CORIN

Into a thousand that I have forgotten.

SILVIUS

O thou didst then never love so heartily,
If thou remember'st not the slightest folly
That ever love did make thee run into,   35
Thou hast not loved.
Or if thou hast not sat as I do now,
Wearing thy hearer in thy mistress' praise,
Thou hast not loved.
Or if thou hast not broke from company,   40

Abruptly as my passion now makes me,
Thou hast not loved.
O Phebe, Phebe, Phebe!   [*Exit.*

ROSALIND

Alas, poor shepherd! Searching of thy wound,
I have by hard adventure found mine own.   45

TOUCHSTONE

And I mine. I remember when I was in love I
broke my sword upon a stone, and bid him take
that for coming a-night to Jane Smile, and I remember the kissing of her batlet, and the cow's
dugs that her pretty chopped hands had milked. 50
And I remember the wooing of a peascod instead
of her, from whom I took two cods, and giving
her them again, said with weeping tears, wear
these for my sake. We that are true lovers run
into strange capers; but as all is mortal in nature, 55
so is all nature in love mortal in folly.

ROSALIND

Thou speak'st wiser than thou art ware of.

TOUCHSTONE

Nay, I shall ne'er be ware of mine own wit, till I
break my shins against it.   60

ROSALIND

Jove, Jove, this shepherd's passion
Is much upon my fashion.

TOUCHSTONE

And mine, but it grows something stale with me.

CELIA

I pray you, one of you question yond man,

If he for gold will give us any food.   65
I faint almost to death.
    TOUCHSTONE
                Holla, you clown!
    ROSALIND
Peace fool, he's not thy kinsman.
    CORIN
                      Who calls?
    TOUCHSTONE
Your betters sir.
    CORIN
            Else are they very wretched.
    ROSALIND
Peace I say. Good even to you friend.
    CORIN
And to you gentle sir, and to you all.   70
    ROSALIND
I prithee shepherd, if that love or gold
Can in this desert place buy entertainment,
Bring us where we may rest ourselves, and feed.
Here's a young maid with travel much oppressed,
And faints for succour. — Nourishment, help aid.
    CORIN
             Fair sir, I pity her,   75
And wish for her sake more than for mine own,
My fortunes were more able to relieve her.
But I am shepherd to another man,
And do not shear the fleeces that I graze.
My master is of <u>churlish</u> disposition,   80
And little recks to find the way to heaven

By doing deeds of hospitality.
Besides, his cote, his flocks, and bounds of feed,
Are now on sale, and at our sheepcote now.
By reason of his absence there is nothing   85
That you will feed on; but what is, come see,
And in my voice most welcome shall you be.

   ROSALIND

What is he that shall buy his flock and pasture?

   CORIN *asks master for cottage*

That young swain that you saw here but erewhile,
That little cares for buying anything.   90

   ROSALIND

I pray thee, if it stand with honesty,
Buy thou the cottage, pasture, and the flock,
And thou shalt have to pay for it of us.

   CELIA *pay you*

And we will mend thy wages. I like this place,
And willingly could waste my time in it.   95

   CORIN

Assuredly the thing is to be sold.
Go with me; if you like, upon report,
The soil, the profit, and this kind of life,
I will your very faithful feeder be,
And buy it with your gold right suddenly.   100

       [*Exeunt.*

Scene five

> *The forest. Enter Amiens, Jaques, and others.*

AMIENS [*sings*]
> *Under the greenwood tree,*
> *Who loves to lie with me,*
> *And turn his merry note*
> *Unto the sweet bird's throat,*
> Come hither, come hither, come hither.   5
> *Here shall he see*
> *No enemy,*
> *But winter and rough weather.*

JAQUES

More, more, I prithee more.

AMIENS

It will make you melancholy Monsieur Jaques.   10

JAQUES

I thank it. More, I prithee more. I can suck melancholy out of a song, as a weasel sucks eggs. More, I prithee more.

AMIENS

My voice is ragged, I know I cannot please you.   15

JAQUES

I do not desire you to please me, I do desire you to sing. Come, more; another stanzo. Call you 'em stanzos?

AMIENS

What you will Monsieur Jaques.   20

JAQUES

Nay, I care not for their names, they owe me
nothing. Will you sing?

AMIENS

More at your request than to please myself.

JAQUES

Well then, if ever I thank any man, I'll thank   25
you; but that they call compliment is like th' encounter of two dog-apes. And when a man
thanks me heartily, methinks I have given him a
penny, and he renders me the beggarly thanks.
Come sing; and you that will not, hold your   30
tongues.

AMIENS

Well, I'll end the song. Sirs, cover the while; the
Duke will drink under this tree. He hath been all
this day to look you.

JAQUES

And I have been all this day to avoid him. He is   35
too disputable for my company. I think of as
many matters as he, but I give heaven thanks,
and make no boast of them. Come, warble,
come.

ALL [*sing*]

  Who doth ambition shun,   40
  And loves to live i' th' sun,
  Seeking the food he eats
  And pleased with what he gets,
Come hither, come hither, come hither.
  Here shall he see   45

         No enemy
    But winter and rough weather.

    JAQUES

I'll give you a verse to this note, that I made
yesterday in despite of my invention.

    AMIENS

And I'll sing it.   50

    JAQUES

Thus it goes.   [*Gives a paper.*

    AMIENS [*sings*]

      If it do come to pass
      That any man turn ass,
      Leaving his wealth and ease,
      A stubborn will to please,   55
  Ducdame, ducdame, ducdame.
        Here shall he see
        Gross fools as he,
   An if he will come to me.

What's that ducdame?   60

    JAQUES

'Tis a Greek invocation, to call fools into a circle. I'll go sleep, if I can; if I cannot, I'll rail
against all the first-born of Egypt.

    AMIENS

And I'll go seek the Duke: his banquet is pre-
pared.   [*Exeunt.*   65

Scene six

The forest. Enter Orlando and Adam.

ADAM

Dear master, I can go no further. O I die for
food. Here lie I down, and measure out my
grave. Farewell kind master.

ORLANDO

Why how now Adam? No greater heart in thee?
Live a little, comfort a little, cheer thyself a lit- 5
tle. If this uncouth forest yield any thing savage,
I will either be food for it, or bring it for food to
thee. Thy conceit is nearer death than thy
powers. For my sake be comfortable; hold death
awhile at the arm's end. I will here be with thee 10
presently, and if I bring thee not something to
eat, I will give thee leave to die; but if thou diest
before I come, thou art a mocker of my labour.
Well said, thou look'st cheerly, and I'll be with
thee quickly. Yet thou liest in the bleak air. 15
Come, I will bear thee to some shelter, and thou
shalt not die for lack of a dinner, if there live
any thing in this desert. Cheerly good Adam.

[Exeunt.

Scene seven

> *The forest. Enter Duke Senior, Amiens, and Lords.*

DUKE SENIOR

I think he be transformed into a beast,
For I can no where find him like a man.

FIRST LORD

My lord, he is but even now gone hence.
Here was he merry, hearing of a song.

DUKE SENIOR

If he, compact of jars, grow musical,   5
We shall have shortly discord in the spheres.
Go seek him, tell him I would speak with him.

> *Enter Jaques.*

FIRST LORD

He saves my labour by his own approach.

DUKE SENIOR

Why how now monsieur, what a life is this,
That your poor friends must woo your company.   10
What, you look merrily.

JAQUES

A fool, a fool! I met a fool i' th' forest,
A motley fool—a miserable world—
As I do live by food, I met a fool,
Who laid him down and basked him in the sun,   15
And railed on Lady Fortune in good terms,
In good set terms, and yet a motley fool.
Good morrow, fool, quoth I. No sir, quoth he,

Jack - Philosophising

Call me not fool till heaven hath sent me fortune.
And then he drew a dial from his poke,   20
And looking on it, with lack-lustre eye,
Says very wisely, it is ten o'clock:
Thus we may see, quoth he, how the world wags.
'Tis but an hour ago since it was nine,
And after one hour more, 'twill be eleven;   25
And so from hour to hour we ripe, and ripe,
And then from hour to hour we rot, and rot;
And thereby hangs a tale. When I did hear
The motley fool thus moral on the time,
My lungs began to crow like chanticleer,   30
That fools should be so deep contemplative.
And I did laugh sans intermission
An hour by his dial. O noble fool,
A worthy fool. Motley's the only wear.

DUKE SENIOR

What fool is this?   35

older + closer to death

JAQUES

O worthy fool. One that hath been a courtier
And says, if ladies be but young and fair,
They have the gift to know it: and in his brain,
Which is as dry as the remainder biscuit
After a voyage, he hath strange places crammed   40
With observation, the which he vents
In mangled forms. O that I were a fool.
I am ambitious for a motley coat.

DUKE SENIOR

Thou shalt have one.

JAQUES

It is my only suit,
Provided that you weed your better judgements   45
Of all opinion that grows rank in them
That I am wise. I must have liberty
Withal, as large a charter as the wind,
To blow on whom I please, for so fools have.
And they that are most galled with my folly,   50
They most must laugh. And why sir must they
    so?
The why is plain as way to parish church.
He that a fool doth very wisely hit
Doth very foolishly, although he smart,
Not to seem senseless of the bob: if not,   55
The wise man's folly is anatomized
Even by the squandering glances of the fool.
Invest me in my motley. Give me leave
To speak my mind, and I will through and
    through
Cleanse the foul body of th' infected world,   60
If they will patiently receive my medicine.

DUKE SENIOR

Fie on thee, I can tell what thou wouldst do.

JAQUES

What, for a counter, would I do but good?

DUKE SENIOR

Most mischievous foul sin, in chiding sin.
For thou thyself hast been a libertine,   65
As sensual as the brutish sting itself,
And all th' imbossed sores, and headed evils,

jack isn't happy in forrest.

That thou with licence of free foot hast caught,
Wouldst thou disgorge into the general world.

      JAQUES

Why who cries out on pride,   70
That can therein tax any private party?
Doth it not flow as hugely as the sea,
Till that the weary very means do ebb?
What woman in the city do I name,
When that I say the city-woman bears   75
The cost of princes on unworthy shoulders?
Who can come in, and say that I mean her,
When such a one as she, such is her neighbour?
Or what is he of basest function,
That says his bravery is not on my cost,   80
Thinking that I mean him, but therein suits
His folly to the mettle of my speech?
There then. How then, what then? Let me see
    wherein
My tongue hath wronged him. If it do him right,
Then he hath wronged himself. If he be free,   85
Why then my taxing like a wild-goose flies
Unclaimed of any man.

     Enter Orlando.

                But who comes here?

     ORLANDO

Forbear, and eat no more.

     JAQUES

              Why I have eat none yet.

     ORLANDO

Nor shalt not, till necessity be served.

JAQUES

Of what kind should this cock come of?   90

DUKE SENIOR

Art thou thus boldened man by thy distress,
Or else a rude despiser of good manners,
That in civility thou seem'st so empty?

ORLANDO

You touched my vein at first; the thorny point
Of bare distress hath ta'en from me the show   95
Of smooth civility. Yet am I inland bred,
And know some nurture. But forbear, I say,
He dies that touches any of this fruit,
Till I and my affairs are answered.

JAQUES

An you will not be answered with reason, I must   100
die.

DUKE SENIOR

What would you have? Your gentleness shall
     force
More than your force move us to gentleness.

ORLANDO

I almost die for food; and let me have it.

DUKE SENIOR

Sit down and feed, and welcome to our table.   105

ORLANDO

Speak you so gently? Pardon me, I pray you;
I thought that all things had been savage here,
And therefore put I on the countenance
Of stern commandment. But whate'er you are

That in this desert inaccessible, 110
Under the shade of melancholy boughs,
Lose and neglect the creeping hours of time.
If ever you have looked on better days,
If ever been where bells have knolled to church,
If ever sat at any good man's feast, 115
If ever from your eyelids wiped a tear,
And know·what 'tis to pity and be pitied,
Let gentleness my strong enforcement be,
In the which hope, I blush, and hide my sword.

DUKE SENIOR

True is it, that we have seen better days, 120
And have with holy bell been knolled to church,
And sat at good men's feasts, and wiped our eyes
Of drops that sacred pity hath engendered.
And therefore sit you down in gentleness,
And take upon command what help we have, 125
That to your wanting may be ministered.

ORLANDO

Then but forbear your food a little while,
Whiles, like a doe, I go to find my fawn,
And give it food. There is an old poor man,
Who after me hath many a weary step 130
Limped in pure love. Till he be first sufficed,
Oppressed with two weak evils, age, and hunger,
I will not touch a bit.

DUKE SENIOR

          Go find him out.
And we will nothing waste till you return.

metaphor.

ORLANDO

I thank ye, and be blessed for your good com-
fort.   [*Exit.* 135

DUKE SENIOR

Thou seest, we are not all alone unhappy.
This wide and universal theatre
Presents more woeful pageants than the scene
Wherein we play in.

JAQUES

*Philosophizing
again*

All the world's a stage,
And all the men and women merely players.   140
They have their exits and their entrances,
And one man in his time plays many parts,
His acts being seven ages. At first the infant,
Crying— Mewling, and puking in the nurse's arms.
Then the whining schoolboy with his satchel   145
And shining morning face, creeping like snail
Unwillingly to school. And then the lover,
Sighing like furnace, with a woeful ballad
Made to his mistress' eyebrow. Then, a soldier,
Full of strange oaths, and bearded like the pard, 150
Jealous in honour, sudden and quick in quarrel,
Seeking the bubble reputation
Even in the cannon's mouth. And then, the jus-
tice,
Chicken
In fair round belly, with good capon lined,
With eyes severe, and beard of formal cut,   155
Full of wise saws and modern instances,
And so he plays his part. The sixth age shifts
Into the lean and slippered pantaloon,

*something given to Justices to pay to
plead cause*

With spectacles on nose, and pouch on side,
His youthful hose well saved, a world too wide   160
For his shrunk shank, and his big manly voice,
Turning again toward childish treble pipes
And whistles in his sound. Last scene of all,
That ends this strange eventful history,
Is second childishness and mere oblivion,   165
Sans teeth, sans eyes, sans taste, sans every
     thing.

>   *Enter Orlando and Adam.*

>   DUKE SENIOR

Welcome. Set down your venerable burthen,
And let him feed.

>   ORLANDO

I thank you most for him.

>   ADAM

>   So had you need,
I scarce can speak to thank you for myself.   170

>   DUKE SENIOR

Welcome, fall to. I will not trouble you
As yet to question you about your fortunes.
Give us some music, and good cousin, sing.

>   AMIENS [*sings*]
>   *Blow, blow, thou winter wind,*
>   *Thou art not so unkind*   175
>   *As man's ingratitude;*
>   *Thy tooth is not so keen,*
>   *Because thou art not seen,*
>   *Although thy breath be rude.*
Heigh-ho, sing heigh-ho, unto the green holly,   180

Most friendship is feigning, most loving mere
          folly.
               Then heigh-ho, the holly,
                    This life is most jolly.

               Freeze, freeze, thou bitter sky,
               That dost not bite so nigh   185
                    As benefits forgot.
               Though thou the waters warp,
               Thy sting is not so sharp
                    As friend remembered not.
Heigh-ho, sing heigh-ho, &c.   190

          DUKE SENIOR

If that you were the good Sir Rowland's son,
As you have whispered faithfully you were,
And as mine eye doth his effigies witness) *likeness*
Most truly limned, and living in your face,
Be truly welcome hither. I am the Duke   195
That loved your father. The residue of your
     fortune,
Go to my cave and tell me. Good old man,
Thou art right welcome as thy master is.
Support him by the arm. Give me your hand,
And let me all your fortunes understand.   200

                                   [*Exeunt.*

——— To here for
     Tues. Oct. 22
               '63

Act three Scene one

          A room in the palace. Enter Duke Fred-
          erick, Lords, and Oliver.

DUKE FREDERICK

Not see him since? Sir, sir, that cannot be.
But were I not the better part made mercy,
I should not seek an absent argument
Of my revenge, thou present. But look to it,
Find out thy brother, wheresoe'er he is.   5
Seek him with candle; bring him dead or living
Within this twelvemonth, or turn thou no more
To seek a living in our territory.
Thy lands and all things that thou dost call thine
Worth seizure, do we seize into our hands,   10
Till thou canst quit thee by thy brother's mouth
Of what we think against thee.

OLIVER

O that your Highness knew my heart in this.
I never loved my brother in my life.

DUKE FREDERICK

More villain thou. Well, push him out of doors,   15
And let my officers of such a nature
Make an extent upon his house and lands.
Do this expediently, and turn him going.

[*Exeunt.*

in a fury

ex – let foot out

Scene two

The forest. Enter Orlando, with a paper.

ORLANDO

Hang there my verse, in witness of my love,
And thou thrice-crowned queen of night survey

With thy chaste eye, from thy pale sphere above,
Thy huntress' name, that my full life doth sway.
O Rosalind, these trees shall be my books,   5
And in their barks my thoughts I'll character,
That every eye, which in this forest looks,
Shall see thy virtue witnessed every where.
Run, run, Orlando, carve on every tree
The fair, the chaste, and unexpressive she. [*Exit.*   10
        Enter Corin and Touchstone.

>   CORIN

And how like you this shepherd's life Master
Touchstone?

>   TOUCHSTONE

Truly shepherd, in respect of itself, it is a good
life; but in respect that it is a shepherd's life, it is   15
naught. In respect that it is solitary, I like it very
well; but in respect that it is private, it is a very
vile life. Now in respect it is in the fields, it pleas-
eth me well; but in respect it is not in the court, it
is tedious. As it is a spare life, look you, it fits my
humour well; but as there is no more plenty in it,   20
it goes much against my stomach. Hast any philosophy in thee shepherd?

>   CORIN

No more, but that I know the more one sickens,
the worse at ease he is; and that he that wants   25
money, means, and content, is without three
good friends. That the property of rain is to wet,
and fire to burn. That good pasture makes fat
sheep; and that a great cause of the night is lack

of the sun. That he that hath learned no wit by   30
nature, nor art, may complain of good breeding,
or comes of a very dull kindred.

TOUCHSTONE

Such a one is a natural philosopher. Wast ever in
court, shepherd?

CORIN

No truly.   35

TOUCHSTONE

Then thou art damned.

CORIN

Nay, I hope.

TOUCHSTONE

Truly thou art damned, like an ill-roasted egg,
all on one side.

CORIN

For not being at court? Your reason?   40

TOUCHSTONE

Why, if thou never wast at court, thou never
saw'st good manners; if thou never saw'st good
manners, then thy manners must be wicked, and
wickedness is sin, and sin is damnation. Thou art
in a parlous state shepherd.   45

CORIN   answer

Not a whit Touchstone; those that are good manners at the court, are as ridiculous in the country,
as the behaviour of the country is most mockable
at the court. You told me, you salute not at the
court, but you kiss your hands; that courtesy   50
would be uncleanly if courtiers were shepherds.

TOUCHSTONE

Instance, briefly; come, instance.

CORIN

Why we are still handling our ewes, and their
fells you know are greasy.   55

TOUCHSTONE

Why do not your courtier's hands sweat? And is
not the grease of a mutton as wholesome as the
sweat of a man? Shallow, shallow. A better instance I say. Come.

CORIN

Besides, our hands are hard.   60

TOUCHSTONE

Your lips will feel them the sooner. Shallow
again; a more sounder instance, come.

CORIN

And they are often tarred over with the surgery
of our sheep; and would you have us kiss tar?
The courtier's hands are perfumed with civet.   65

TOUCHSTONE

Most shallow man. Thou worms-meat in respect
of a good piece of flesh indeed. Learn of the wise
and perpend. Civet is of a baser birth than tar,
the very uncleanly flux of a cat. Mend the in-   70
stance shepherd.

CORIN

You have too courtly a wit for me, I'll rest.

TOUCHSTONE

Wilt thou rest damned? God help thee shallow
man. God make incision in thee, thou art raw.   75

CORIN

Sir, I am a true labourer; I earn that I eat; get that I wear; owe no man hate, envy no man's happiness; glad of other men's good, content with my harm; and the greatest of my pride, is to see my ewes graze and my lambs suck. 80

TOUCHSTONE

That is another simple sin in you, to bring the ewes and the rams together, and to offer to get your living by the copulation of cattle; to be bawd to a bell-wether, and to betray a she-lamb 85 of a twelvemonth to a crooked-pated old cuck-oldly ram, out of all reasonable match. If thou beest not damned for this, the devil himself will have no shepherds, I cannot see else how thou shoudst 'scape. 90

CORIN

Here comes young Master Ganymede, my new mistress's brother.

Enter Rosalind, with a paper.

ROSALIND

From the east to western Ind,
No jewel is like Rosalind.
Her worth being mounted on the wind, 95
Through all the world bears Rosalind.
All the pictures fairest lined
Are but black to Rosalind.
Let no face be kept in mind
But the fair of Rosalind. 100

TOUCHSTONE

I'll rhyme you so, eight years together, dinners,
and suppers, and sleeping-hours excepted: it is
the right butter-women's rank to market.

ROSALIND

Out fool!   105

TOUCHSTONE

For a taste.

> *If a hart do lack a hind,*
> *Let him seek out Rosalind.*
> *If the cat will after kind,*
> *So be sure will Rosalind.*   110
> *Wintered garments must be lined,*
> *So must slender Rosalind.*
> *They that reap must sheaf and bind,*
> *Then to cart with Rosalind.*
> *Sweetest nut hath sourest rind,*   115
> *Such a nut is Rosalind.*
> *He that sweetest rose will find,*
> *Must find love's prick, and Rosalind.*

This is the very false gallop of verses, why do you
infect yourself with them?   120

ROSALIND

Peace you dull fool, I found them on a tree.

TOUCHSTONE

Truly the tree yields bad fruit.

ROSALIND

I'll graff it with you, and then I shall graff it
with a medlar. Then it will be the earliest fruit
i' th' country; for you'll be rotten ere you be half   125

ripe, and that's the right virtue of the medlar.

>TOUCHSTONE

You have said; but whether wisely or no, let the
forest judge.   130

>*Enter Celia, with a paper.*

>ROSALIND

Peace, here comes my sister, reading, stand
aside.

>CELIA

>*Why should this a desert be?*
>*For it is unpeopled? No.*
>*Tongues I'll hang on every tree,*   135
>*That shall civil sayings show.*
>*Some, how brief the life of man*
>*Runs his erring pilgrimage,*
>*That the stretching of a span*
>*Buckles in his sum of age.*   140
>*Some, of violated vows*
>*'Twixt the souls of friend and friend.*
>*But upon the fairest boughs,*
>*Or at every sentence end,*
>*Will I Rosalinda write,*   145
>*Teaching all that read to know*
>*The quintessence of every sprite*
>*Heaven would in little show.*
>*Therefore Heaven Nature charged*
>*That one body should be filled*   150
>*With all graces wide-enlarged.*
>*Nature presently distilled*
>*Helen's cheek, but not her heart;*

> Cleopatra's majesty;
> Atalanta's better part;   155
>   Sad Lucretia's modesty. —
> Thus Rosalind of many parts
>   By heavenly synod was devised,
> Of many faces, eyes, and hearts,
>   To have the touches dearest prized.   160
Heaven would that she these gifts should have,
And I to live and die her slave.

ROSALIND

O most gentle Jupiter, what tedious homily of
love have you wearied your parishioners withal,
and never cried, have patience good people.   165

CELIA

How now? Back, friends. Shepherd, go off a
little. Go with him sirrah.

TOUCHSTONE

Come shepherd, let us make an honourable re-
treat, though not with bag and baggage, yet with   170
scrip and scrippage.

[*Exeunt Corin and Touchstone.*

CELIA

Didst thou hear these verses?

ROSALIND

O yes, I heard them all, and more too, for some
of them had in them more feet than the verses
would bear.   175

CELIA

That's no matter; the feet might bear the verses.

ROSALIND

Ay, but the feet were lame, and could not bear
themselves without the verse, and therefore stood
lamely in the verse.   180

CELIA

But didst thou hear without wondering, how thy
name should be hanged and carved upon these
trees?

ROSALIND

I was seven of the nine days out of the wonder,
before you came; for look here what I found on a   185
palm-tree; I was never so berhymed since Pythagoras' time that I was an Irish rat, which I
can hardly remember.

CELIA

Trow you, who hath done this?

ROSALIND

Is it a man?   190

CELIA

And a chain that you once wore about his neck.
Change you colour?

ROSALIND

I prithee who?

CELIA

O lord, lord, it is a hard matter for friends to
meet; but mountains may be removed with   195
earthquakes, and so encounter.

ROSALIND

Nay, but who is it?

CELIA

Is it possible?

ROSALIND

Nay, I prithee now, with most petitionary vehe-
mence, tell me who it is.   200

CELIA

O wonderful, wonderful, and most wonderful
wonderful, and yet again wonderful, and after
that out of all whooping.

ROSALIND

Good my complexion, dost thou think though I
am caparisoned like a man, I have a doublet and   205
hose in my disposition? One inch of delay more
is a South-sea of discovery. I prithee tell me who
is it quickly, and speak apace. I would thou
couldst stammer, that thou might'st pour this
concealed man out of thy mouth, as wines comes   210
out of a narrow-mouthed bottle—either too
much at once, or none at all. I prithee take the
cork out of thy mouth, that I may drink thy tidings.

CELIA

So you may put a man in your belly.   215

ROSALIND

Is he of God's making? What manner of man? Is
his head worth a hat? Or his chin worth a
beard?

CELIA

Nay, he hath but a little beard.

ROSALIND

Why God will send more, if the man will be 220
thankful. Let me stay the growth of his beard, if
thou delay me not the knowledge of his chin.

CELIA

It is young Orlando, that tripped up the wrestler's heels and your heart, both in an instant. 225

ROSALIND

Nay, but the devil take mocking. Speak sad
brow, and true maid.

CELIA

I' faith, coz, 'tis he.

ROSALIND

Orlando?

CELIA

Orlando. 230

ROSALIND

Alas the day, what shall I do with my doublet
and hose? What did he when thou saw'st him?
What said he? How looked he? Wherein went
he? What makes he here? Did he ask for me?
Where remains he? How parted he with thee? 235
And when shalt thou see him again? Answer me
in one word.

CELIA

You must borrow me Gargantua's mouth first:
'tis a word too great for any mouth of this age's
size. To say ay and no to these particulars is 240
more than to answer in a catechism.

ROSALIND

But doth he know that I am in this forest, and in man's apparel? Looks he as freshly as he did the day he wrestled?

CELIA

It is as easy to count atomies as to resolve the 245 propositions of a lover. But take a taste of my finding him, and relish it with good observance. I found him under a tree like a dropped acorn.

ROSALIND

It may well be called Jove's tree, when it drops such fruit. 250

CELIA

Give me audience, good madam.

ROSALIND

Proceed.

CELIA

There lay he stretched along like a wounded knight.

ROSALIND

Though it be pity to see such a sight, it well be- 255 comes the ground.

CELIA

Cry holla to the tongue, I prithee; it curvets unseasonably. He was furnished like a hunter.

ROSALIND

O ominous, he comes to kill my heart. 260

CELIA

I would sing my song without a burthen, thou

bring'st me out of tune.

ROSALIND

Do you not know I am a woman? When I think,
I must speak. Sweet, say on.

CELIA

You bring me out.

Enter Orlando and Jaques.

Soft, comes he not here?   265

ROSALIND

'Tis he, slink by, and note him.

[*Celia and Rosalind retire.*

JAQUES

I thank you for your company, but good faith I
had as lief have been myself alone.   270

ORLANDO

And so had I. But yet for fashion sake I thank
you too, for your society.

JAQUES

God b' wi' you, let's meet as little as we can.

ORLANDO

I do desire we may be better strangers.   275

JAQUES

I pray you mar no more trees with writing love-
songs in their barks.

ORLANDO

I pray you mar no moe of my verses with reading
them ill-favouredly.

JAQUES

Rosalind is your love's name?   280

ORLANDO

Yes, just.

JAQUES

I do not like her name.

ORLANDO

There was no thought of pleasing you when she
was christened.

JAQUES

What stature is she of?   285

ORLANDO

Just as high as my heart.

JAQUES

You are full of pretty answers. Have you not
been acquainted with goldsmiths' wives, and
conned them out of rings?

ORLANDO

Not so; but I answer you right painted cloth,   290
from whence you have studied your questions.

JAQUES

You have a nimble wit. I think 'twas made of
Atalanta's heels. Will you sit down with me, and
we two will rail against our mistress the world,   295
and all our misery.

ORLANDO

I will chide no breather in the world but myself
against whom I know most faults.

JAQUES

The worst fault you have, is to be in love.   300

ORLANDO

'Tis a fault I will not change for your best virtue.

Beautiful maiden known for
beauty & speed in running

I am weary of you.

JAQUES

By my troth, I was seeking for a fool, when I found you.

ORLANDO

He is drowned in the brook, look but in, and you 305 shall see him.

JAQUES

There I shall see mine own figure.

ORLANDO

Which I take to be either a fool, or a cipher.

JAQUES

I'll tarry no longer with you; farewell good Signior Love.   310

ORLANDO

I am glad of your departure. Adieu good Monsieur Melancholy.   [*Exit Jaques.*

ROSALIND [*aside to Celia*]

I will speak to him like a saucy lackey, and under that habit play the knave with him. Do you hear forester?   315

ORLANDO

Very well. What would you?

ROSALIND

I pray you, what is't a clock?

ORLANDO

You should ask me what time o' day. There's no clock in the forest.   320

ROSALIND

Then there is no true lover in the forest, else

sighing every minute, and groaning every hour, would detect the lazy foot of Time, as well as a clock.

ORLANDO

And why not the swift foot of Time? Had not that been as proper?   325

ROSALIND

By no means sir. Time travels in divers paces, with divers persons. I'll tell you who Time ambles withal, who Time trots withal, who Time gallops withal, and who he stands still withal.

ORLANDO

I prithee, who doth he trot withal?   330

ROSALIND

Marry he trots hard with a young maid between the contract of her marriage, and the day it is solemnized. If the interim be but a se'nnight, Time's pace is so hard that it seems the length of seven year.   335

ORLANDO

Who ambles Time withal?

ROSALIND

With a priest that lacks Latin, and a rich man that hath not the gout. For the one sleeps easily because he cannot study, and the other lives merrily, because he feels no pain; the one lack-   340
ing the burthen of lean and wasteful learning; the other knowing no burthen of heavy tedious penury. These Time ambles withal.

ORLANDO

Who doth he gallop withal?

ROSALIND

With a thief to the gallows. For though he go as   345
softly as foot can fall, he thinks himself too soon
there.

ORLANDO

Who stays it still withal?

ROSALIND

With lawyers in the vacation. For they sleep between term and term, and then they perceive not   350
how Time moves.

ORLANDO

Where dwell you pretty youth?

ROSALIND

With this shepherdess my sister: here in the skirts
of the forest, like fringe upon a petticoat.   355

ORLANDO

Are you native of this place?

ROSALIND

As the cony that you see dwell where she is kin-
dled.

ORLANDO

Your accent is something finer than you could
purchase in so removed a dwelling.   360

ROSALIND

I have been told so of many. But indeed, an old
religious uncle of mine taught me to speak, who
was in his youth an inland man, one that knew
courtship too well, for there he fell in love. I

have heard him read many lectures against it, 365
and, I thank God, I am not a woman, to be
touched with so many giddy offences as he hath
generally taxed their whole sex withal.

ORLANDO

Can you remember any of the principal evils that
he laid to the charge of women? 370

ROSALIND

There were none principal, they were all like
one another as half-pence are, every one fault
seeming monstrous, till his fellow-fault came to
match it.

ORLANDO

I prithee recount some of them. 375

ROSALIND

No, I will not cast away my physic but on those
that are sick. There is a man haunts the forest,
that abuses our young plants with carving Rosalind on their barks; hangs odes upon hawthorns,
and elegies on brambles; all, forsooth, deifying 380
the name of Rosalind. If I could meet that fancy-
monger, I would give him some good counsel,
for he seems to have the quotidian of love upon
him.

ORLANDO

I am he that is so love-shaked. I pray you tell me 385
your remedy.

ROSALIND

There is none of my uncle's marks upon you. He
taught me how to know a man in love; in which

cage of rushes I am sure you are not prisoner.   390

ORLANDO

What were his marks?

ROSALIND

A lean cheek, which you have not; a blue eye
and sunken, which you have not; an unquestionable spirit, which you have not; a beard neg-
lected, which you have not—but I pardon you   395
for that, for simply your having in beard is a
younger brother's revenue—then your hose
should be ungartered, your bonnet unbanded,
your sleeve unbuttoned, your shoe untied, and
every thing about you demonstrating a careless
desolation. But you are no such man: you are   400
rather point-device in your accoutrements, as
loving yourself, than seeming the lover of any
other.

ORLANDO

Fair youth, I would I could make thee believe
I love.   405

ROSALIND

Me believe it? You may as soon make her that
you love believe it, which I warrant she is apter
to do than to confess she does. That is one of the
points in the which women still give the lie to
their consciences. But in good sooth, are you he   410
that hangs the verses on the trees, wherein Rosalind is so admired?

ORLANDO

I swear to thee youth, by the white hand of

Rosalind, I am that he, that unfortunate he.   415

ROSALIND

But are you so much in love as your rhymes speak?

ORLANDO

Neither rhyme nor reason can express how much.

ROSALIND

Love is merely a madness, and I tell you, de-   420
serves as well a dark house and a whip as mad-
men do; and the reason why they are not so pun-
ished and cured is, that the lunacy is so ordinary, that the whippers are in love too. Yet I pro-
fess curing it by counsel.   425

ORLANDO

Did you ever cure any so?

ROSALIND

Yes, one, and in this manner. He was to imagine
me his love, his mistress; and I set him every day
to woo me. At which time would I, being but a
moonish youth, grieve, be effeminate, change-   430
able, longing, and liking, proud, fantastical,
apish, shallow, inconstant, full of tears, full of
smiles; for every passion something, and for no
passion truly any thing, as boys and women are
for the most part cattle of this colour; would now   435
like him, now loathe him; then entertain him,
then forswear him; now weep for him, then spit
at him; that I drave my suitor from his mad
humour of love to a living humour of madness,

which was to forswear the full stream of the 440
world, and to live in a nook merely monastic.
And thus I cured him, and this way will I take
upon me to wash your liver as clean as a sound
sheep's heart, that there shall not be one spot of
love in't. 445

ORLANDO

I would not be cured, youth.

ROSALIND

I would cure you, if you would but call me Rosalind, and come every day to my cote, and woo
me.

ORLANDO

Now by the faith of my love, I will. Tell me
where it is. 450

ROSALIND

Go with me to it, and I'll show it you. And by
the way you shall tell me where in the forest you
live. Will you go?

ORLANDO

With all my heart, good youth.

ROSALIND

Nay, you must call me Rosalind. Come sister, 455
will you go?   [*Exeunt.*

Scene three

> *The forest. Enter Touchstone and Au-*
> *drey; Jaques following.*

TOUCHSTONE

Come apace good Audrey, I will fetch up your
goats, Audrey. And how, Audrey? Am I the
man yet? Doth my simple feature content you?

AUDREY

Your features? Lord warrant us, what features?   5

TOUCHSTONE

I am here with thee and thy goats, as the most
capricious poet, honest Ovid, was among the
Goths.

JAQUES [*aside*]

O knowledge ill-inhabited, worse than Jove in a   10
thatched house.

TOUCHSTONE

When a man's verses cannot be understood, nor
a man's good wit seconded with the forward
child, understanding, it strikes a man more dead
than a great reckoning in a little room. Truly, I   15
would the gods had made thee poetical.

AUDREY

I do not know what poetical is. Is it honest in
deed and word? Is it a true thing?

TOUCHSTONE

No truly; for the truest poetry is the most feigning, and lovers are given to poetry; and what   20
they swear in poetry may be said as lovers they
do feign.

AUDREY

Do you wish then that the gods had made me
poetical?

TOUCHSTONE

I do truly: for thou swear'st to me thou art hon- 25
est. Now if thou wert a poet, I might have some
hope thou didst feign.

AUDREY

Would you not have me honest?

TOUCHSTONE

No truly, unless thou wert hard-favoured; for
honesty coupled to beauty, is to have honey a 30
sauce to sugar.

JAQUES [*aside*]

A material fool.

AUDREY

Well, I am not fair, and therefore I pray the gods
make me honest.

TOUCHSTONE

Truly, and to cast away honesty upon a foul 35
slut, were to put good meat into an unclean dish.

AUDREY

I am not a slut, though I thank the gods I am
foul.

TOUCHSTONE

Well, praised be the gods for thy foulness; slut- 40
tishness may come hereafter. But be it as it may
be, I will marry thee. And to that end I have
been with Sir Oliver Martext, the vicar of the
next village, who hath promised to meet me in
this place of the forest, and to couple us. 45

JAQUES [*aside*]

I would fain see this meeting.

AUDREY

Well, the gods give us joy!

TOUCHSTONE

Amen. A man may, if he were of a fearful heart, stagger in this attempt; for here we have no temple but the wood, no assembly but horn-beasts. But what though? Courage! As horns are odious, they are necessary. It is said, many a man knows no end of his goods; right. Many a man has good horns, and knows no end of them. Well, that is the dowry of his wife, 'tis none of his own getting. Horns! Even so poor men alone. No, no; the noblest deer hath them as huge as the rascal. Is the single man therefore blessed? No, as a walled town is more worthier than a village, so is the forehead of a married man more honourable than the bare brow of a bachelor. And by how much defence is better than no skill, by so much is a horn more precious than to want.

Enter Sir Oliver Martext.

Here comes Sir Oliver. Sir Oliver Martext, you are well met. Will you dispatch us here under this tree, or shall we go with you to your chapel?

MARTEXT

Is there none here to give the woman?

TOUCHSTONE

I will not take her on gift of any man.

MARTEXT

Truly she must be given, or the marriage is not

lawful.

JAQUES [*comes forward*]

Proceed, proceed. I'll give her.

TOUCHSTONE

Good even good Master What-ye-call't. How do
you sir; you are very well met. God 'ild you for
your last company; I am very glad to see you;
even a toy in hand here sir. Nay, pray be covered.

JAQUES

Will you be married, motley?

TOUCHSTONE

As the ox hath his bow sir, the horse his curb,
and the falcon her bells, so man hath his desires,
and as pigeons bill, so wedlock would be nib-
bling.

JAQUES

And will you, being a man of your breeding, be
married under a bush like a beggar? Get you to
church, and have a good priest that can tell you
what marriage is; this fellow will but join you together as they join wainscot; then one of you will
prove a shrunk panel, and like green timber,
warp, warp.

TOUCHSTONE [*aside*]

I am not in the mind; but I were better to be
married of him than of another, for he is not like
to marry me well; and not being well married,
it will be a good excuse for me hereafter, to
leave my wife.

JAQUES
Go thou with me, and let me counsel thee.

TOUCHSTONE
Come sweet Audrey,
We must be married, or we must live in bawdry.
Farewell good Master Oliver; not [*sings*]   100

       O sweet Oliver,
       O brave Oliver,
    Leave me not behind thee;

but—

       Wind away,   105
       Be gone I say,
  I will not to wedding with thee,
        [*Exeunt Jaques, Touch-
        stone, and Audrey.*

MARTEXT
'Tis no matter. Ne'er a fantastical knave of them
all shall flout me out of my calling.   [*Exit.*

Scene four   Orlando is late · she cries

    The forest. Enter Rosalind and Celia.

ROSALIND
Never talk to me, I will weep.

CELIA
Do I prithee, but yet have the grace to consider
that tears do not become a man.

ROSALIND
But have I not cause to weep?

CELIA

As good cause as one would desire, therefore 5
weep.

ROSALIND

His very hair is of the dissembling colour. *treacherous*
red hair—

CELIA

Something browner than Judas's; marry his
kisses are Judas's own children. 10

ROSALIND

I' faith his hair is of a good colour.

CELIA

An excellent colour; your chestnut was ever the
only colour.

ROSALIND

And his kissing is as full of sanctity as the touch
of holy bread. 15

CELIA

He hath bought a pair of cast lips of Diana. A
nun of winter's sisterhood kisses not more re-
ligiously, the very ice of chastity is in them.

ROSALIND *(primly)*

But why did he swear he would come this morn- 20
ing, and comes not?

CELIA

Nay certainly there is no truth in him.

ROSALIND

Do you think so?

CELIA

Yes, I think he is not a pick-purse nor a horse-
stealer, but for his verity in love, I do think him 25
(truth)

as concave as a covered goblet or a worm-eaten
nut.

Simile

ROSALIND

Not true in love?

CELIA

Yes, when he is in, but I think he is not in.   30

ROSALIND

You have heard him swear downright he was.

CELIA

Was, is not is. Besides, the oath of a lover is no
stronger than the word of a tapster; they are
both the confirmer of false reckonings. He at-   35
tends here in the forest on the Duke your father.

ROSALIND

I met the Duke yesterday, and had much question with him. He asked me, of what parentage
I was. I told him, of as good as he, so he laughed   40
and let me go. But what talk we of fathers, when
there is such a man as Orlando?

CELIA

O that's a brave man, he writes brave verses,
speaks brave words, swears brave oaths, and
breaks them bravely, quite traverse athwart the   45
heart of his lover, as a puisny tilter that spurs his
horse but on one side breaks his staff like a noble
goose. But all's brave that youth mounts, and
folly guides. Who comes here?

Enter Corin.

CORIN — *shepherd – laugh them a cottage*

Mistress and master, you have oft enquired   50

After the shepherd that complained of love,
Who you saw sitting by me on the turf,
Praising the proud disdainful shepherdess
That was his mistress.

CELIA

        Well, and what of him?

CORIN

If you will see a pageant truly played.   55
Between the pale complexion of true love,
And the red glow of scorn and proud disdain,
Go hence a little, and I shall conduct you
If you will mark it.

ROSALIND

        O come, let us remove.
The sight of lovers feedeth those in love.   60
Bring us to this sight, and you shall say
I'll prove a busy actor in their play.   [*Exeunt.*

Scene five

     The forest. Enter Silvius and Phebe.

SILVIUS

Sweet Phebe do not scorn me, do not Phebe.
Say that you love me not, but say not so
In bitterness. The common executioner,
Whose heart th' accustomed sight of death makes
    hard,
Falls not the axe upon the humbled neck   5
But first begs pardon. Will you sterner be

Than he that dies and lives by bloody drops?
> *Enter Rosalind, Celia, and Corin behind.*

PHEBE

I would not be thy executioner.
I fly thee, for I would not injure thee.
Thou tell'st me there is murder in mine eye,   10
'Tis pretty, sure, and very probable,
That eyes, that are the frail'st and softest things,
Who shut their coward gates on atomies,
Should be called tyrants, butchers, murderers.
Now I do frown on thee with all my heart,   15
And if mine eyes can wound now let them kill
   thee.
Now counterfeit to swoon, why now fall down,
Or if thou canst not, o for shame, for shame,
Lie not, to say mine eyes are murderers.
Now show the wound mine eye hath made in
   thee.   20
Scratch thee but with a pin, and there remains
Some scar of it. Lean upon a rush,
The cicatrice and capable impressure
Thy palm some moment keeps. But now mine
   eyes
Which I have darted at thee hurt thee not,   25
Nor I am sure there is no force in eyes
That can do hurt.

SILVIUS
          O dear Phebe,
If ever—as that ever may be near—

You meet in some fresh cheek the power of
    fancy,
Then shall you know the wounds invisible   30
That love's keen arrows make.

    PHEBE

                    But till that time
Come not thou near me. And when that time
    comes,
Afflict me with thy mocks, pity me not,
As till that time I shall not pity thee.

    ROSALIND

And why I pray you? Who might be your
    mother,   35
That you insult, exult, and all at once,
Over the wretched? What though you have no
    beauty—
As by my faith I see no more in you
Than without candle may go dark to bed—
Must you be therefore proud and pitiless?   40
Why what means this? Why do you look on me?
I see no more in you than in the ordinary
Of nature's sale-work. 'Ods my little life,
I think she means to tangle my eyes too.
No faith proud mistress, hope not after it.   45
'Tis not your inky brows, your black silk hair,
Your bugle eyeballs, nor your cheek of cream,
That can entame my spirits to your worship.
You foolish shepherd, wherefore do you follow
    her,
Like foggy south puffing with wind and rain?   50

You are a thousand times a properer man
Than she a woman. 'Tis such fools as you
That makes the world full of ill-favoured
    children.
'Tis not her glass, but you, that flatters her,
And out of you she sees herself more proper   55
Than any of her lineaments can show her.
But mistress, know yourself, down on your
    knees,
And thank heaven, fasting, for a good man's
    love.
For I must tell you friendly in your ear,
Sell when you can, you are not for all markets.   60
Cry the man mercy, love him, take his offer.
Foul is most foul, being foul to be a scoffer.
So take her to thee shepherd, fare you well.

    PHEBE

Sweet youth, I pray you chide a year together,
I had rather hear you chide than this man woo.   65

    ROSALIND [*aside*]

He's fallen in love with your foulness, and she'll
fall in love with my anger. If it be so, as fast as
she answers thee with frowning looks, I'll sauce
her with bitter words. [*To Phebe.*] Why look you
so upon me?   70

    PHEBE

For no ill will I bear you.

    ROSALIND

I pray you do not fall in love with me,
For I am falser than vows made in wine.

Hero & Leander

Besides, I like you not. If you will know my
    house,
'Tis at the tuft of olives, here hard by.   75
Will you go sister? Shepherd, ply her hard.
Come sister. Shepherdess, look on him better
And be not proud, though all the world could
    see,
None could be so abused in sight as he.
Come, to our flock.   80
       [*Exeunt Rosalind, Celia, and Corin.*

    PHEBE
Dead shepherd, now I find thy saw of might,
Who ever loved that loved not at first sight?
    SILVIUS
Sweet Phebe—
    PHEBE
           Ha, what sayst thou Silvius?
    SILVIUS
Sweet Phebe pity me.
    PHEBE
Why I am sorry for thee gentle Silvius.   85
    SILVIUS
Wherever sorrow is, relief would be.
If you do sorrow at my grief in love,
By giving love your sorrow and my grief
Were both extermined.
    PHEBE
Thou hast my love, is not that neighbourly?   90
    SILVIUS
I would have you.

PHEBE

Why that were covetousness.
Silvius, the time was, that I hated thee;
And yet it is not, that I bear thee love.
But since that thou canst talk of love so well,
Thy company, which erst was irksome to me,   95
I will endure; and I'll employ thee too.
But do not look for further recompense
Than thine own gladness that thou art employed.

SILVIUS

So holy and so perfect is my love,
And I in such a poverty of grace,   100
That I shall think it a most plenteous crop
To glean the broken ears after the man
That the main harvest reaps. Loose now and then
A scattered smile, and that I'll live upon.

PHEBE

Know'st thou the youth that spoke to me ere-
    while?   105

SILVIUS

Not very well, but I have met him oft,
And he hath bought the cottage and the bounds
That the old carlot once was master of.

PHEBE

Think not I love him, though I ask for him;
'Tis but a peevish boy, yet he talks well.   110
But what care I for words? Yet words do well
When he that speaks them pleases those that
    hear.
It is a pretty youth, not very pretty,

But sure he's proud, and yet his pride becomes
   him.
He'll make a proper man. The best thing in him   115
Is his complexion. And faster than his tongue
Did make offence, his eye did heal it up.
He is not very tall, yet for his years he's tall.
His leg is but so so, and yet 'tis well.
There was a pretty redness in his lip,   120
A little riper, and more lusty red
Than that mixed in his cheek. 'Twas just the
   difference
Betwixt the constant red and mingled damask.
There be some women Silvius, had they marked
   him
In parcels as I did, would have gone near   125
To fall in love with him. But for my part
I love him not, nor hate him not. And yet
I have more cause to hate him than to love him,
For what had he to do to chide at me?
He said mine eyes were black, and my hair
   black,   130
And now I am remembered, scorned at me.
I marvel why I answered not again,
But that's all one. Omittance is no quittance.
I'll write to him a very taunting letter,
And thou shalt bear it, wilt thou Silvius?   135
      SILVIUS
Phebe, with all my heart.
      PHEBE
                      I'll write it straight.

The matter's in my head, and in my heart.
I will be bitter with him, and passing short.
Go with me Silvius.   [*Exeunt.*

Act four Scene one

> *The forest. Enter Rosalind, Celia, and
> Jaques.*

JAQUES

I prithee, pretty youth, let me be better acquainted with thee.

ROSALIND

They say you are a melancholy fellow.

JAQUES

I am so. I do love it better than laughing.

ROSALIND

Those that are in extremity of either are abominable fellows, and betray themselves to every modern censure, worse than drunkards.   5

JAQUES

Why, 'tis good to be sad and say nothing.

ROSALIND

Why then 'tis good to be a post.

JAQUES

I have neither the scholar's melancholy, which is emulation; nor the musician's, which is fantastical; nor the courtier's, which is proud; nor the soldier's, which is ambitious; nor the lawyer's, which is politic; nor the lady's, which is nice; nor   10

the lover's, which is all these; but it is a melan- 15
choly of mine own, compounded of many sim-
ples, extracted from many objects, and indeed
the sundry contemplation of my travels, in which
my often rumination wraps me in a most humorous sadness. 20

ROSALIND

A traveller? By my faith, you have great reason
to be sad. I fear you have sold your own lands, to
see other men's; then to have seen much, and to
have nothing, is to have rich eyes and poor
hands. 25

JAQUES

Yes, I have gained my experience.

ROSALIND

And your experience makes you sad. I had rather
have a fool to make me merry than experience to
make me sad—and to travel for it too.

Enter Orlando.

ORLANDO

Good day and happiness, dear Rosalind. 30

JAQUES

Nay then God b' wi' you, an you talk in blank
verse. [*Exit.*

ROSALIND

Farewell Monsieur Traveller: look you lisp, and
wear strange suits; disable all the benefits of your
own country; be out of love with your nativity, 35
and almost chide God for making you that countenance you are; or I will scarce think you have

swam in a gondola. Why how now Orlando,
where have you been all this while? You a lover?
An you serve me such another trick, never come 40
in my sight more.

ORLANDO

My fair Rosalind, I come within an hour of my
promise.

ROSALIND

Break an hour's promise in love? He that will
divide a minute into a thousand parts, and break 45
but a part of the thousandth part of a minute in
the affairs of love, it may be said of him that
Cupid hath clapped him o' th' shoulder, but I'll
warrant him heart-whole.

ORLANDO

Pardon me dear Rosalind. 50

ROSALIND

Nay, an you be so tardy, come no more in my
sight. I had as lief be wooed of a snail.

ORLANDO

Of a snail?

ROSALIND

Ay, of a snail. For though he comes slowly, he
carries his house on his head, a better jointure 55
I think than you make a woman; besides, he
brings his destiny with him.

ORLANDO

What's that?

ROSALIND

Why horns, which such as you are fain to be be-

holding to your wives for. But he comes armed 60
in his fortune, and prevents the slander of his
wife.

ORLANDO

Virtue is no horn-maker; and my Rosalind is
virtuous.

ROSALIND

And I am your Rosalind. 65

CELIA

It pleases him to call you so. But he hath a Rosalind of a better leer than you.

ROSALIND

Come, woo me, woo me; for now I am in a holiday humour, and like enough to consent. What
would you say to me now, an I were your very, 70
very Rosalind?

ORLANDO

I would kiss before I spoke.

ROSALIND

Nay, you were better speak first, and when you
were gravelled, for lack of matter, you might take
occasion to kiss. Very good orators, when they 75
are out, they will spit, and for lovers, lacking—
God warn us—matter, the cleanliest shift is to
kiss.

ORLANDO

How if the kiss be denied? *request*

ROSALIND

Then she puts you to entreaty, and there begins 80
new matter.

ORLANDO

Who could be out, being before his beloved mistress?

ROSALIND

Marry that should you, if I were your mistress, or I should think my honesty ranker than my wit. 85

ORLANDO

What, of my suit?

ROSALIND

Not out of your apparel, and yet out of your suit. Am not I your Rosalind?

ORLANDO

I take some joy to say you are, because I would 90 be talking of her.

ROSALIND

Well, in her person, I say I will not have you.

ORLANDO

Then in mine own person, I die.

ROSALIND

No faith, die by attorney. The poor world is almost six thousand years old, and in all this time 95 there was not any man died in his own person, videlicet, in a love-cause. Troilus had his brains dashed out with a Grecian club, yet he did what he could to die before, and he is one of the patterns of love. Leander, he would have lived many 100 a fair year though Hero had turned nun, if it had not been for a hot midsummer night; for, good youth, he went but forth to wash him in the Hellespont, and being taken with the cramp, was

drowned, and the foolish chroniclers of that age 105
found it was Hero of Sestos. But these are all lies;
men have died from time to time, and worms
have eaten them, but not for love.

ORLANDO

I would not have my right Rosalind of this mind,
for I protest her frown might kill me. 110

ROSALIND

By this hand, it will not kill a fly. But come, now
I will be your Rosalind in a more coming-on disposition; and ask me what you will, I will grant
it.

ORLANDO

Then love me Rosalind. 115

ROSALIND

Yes faith will I, Fridays and Saturdays, and all.

ORLANDO

And wilt thou have me?

ROSALIND

Ay, and twenty such.

ORLANDO

What sayest thou? 120

ROSALIND

Are you not good?

ORLANDO

I hope so.

ROSALIND

Why then, can one desire too much of a good
thing? Come sister, you shall be the priest, and
marry us. Give me your hand Orlando. What do 125

you say sister?

ORLANDO

Pray thee marry us.

CELIA

I cannot say the words.

ROSALIND

You must begin, will you Orlando——

CELIA

Go to. Will you Orlando, have to wife this Rosa-   130
lind?

ORLANDO

I will.

ROSALIND

Ay, but when?

ORLANDO

Why now, as fast as she can marry us.

ROSALIND

Then you must say, I take thee Rosalind for wife.   135

ORLANDO

I take thee Rosalind for wife.

ROSALIND

I might ask you for your commission, but I do
take thee Orlando for my husband. There's a girl
goes before the priest, and certainly a woman's   140
thought runs before her actions.

ORLANDO

So do all thoughts, they are winged.

ROSALIND

Now tell me how long you would have her, after
you have possessed her.

ORLANDO

For ever, and a day.   145

ROSALIND

Say a day, without the ever. No, no, Orlando,
men are April when they woo, December when
they wed. Maids are May when they are maids,
but the sky changes when they are wives. I will
be more jealous of thee than a Barbary cock-   150
pigeon over his hen, more clamorous than a par-
rot against rain, more new-fangled than an ape,
more giddy in my desires than a monkey. I will
weep for nothing, like Diana in the fountain, and
I will do that when you are disposed to be merry.   155
I will laugh like a hyen, and that when thou art
inclined to sleep.

ORLANDO

But will my Rosalind do so?

ROSALIND

By my life, she will do as I do.

ORLANDO

O but she is wise.   160

ROSALIND

Or else she could not have the wit to do this. The
wiser, the waywarder. Make the doors upon a
woman's wit, and it will out at the casement. Shut
that, and 'twill out at the key-hole. Stop that,
'twill fly with the smoke out at the chimney.   165

ORLANDO

A man that had a wife with such a wit, he might
say, wit whither wilt? *fantastic speech*

ROSALIND

Nay, you might keep that check for it, till you
met your wife's wit going to your neighbour's   170
bed.

ORLANDO

And what wit could wit have, to excuse that?

ROSALIND

Marry to say, she came to seek you there. You
shall never take her without her answer, unless   175
you take her without her tongue. O that woman
that cannot make her fault her husband's occasion, let her never nurse her child herself, for she
will breed it like a fool.

ORLANDO

For these two hours Rosalind, I will leave thee.   180

ROSALIND

Alas, dear love, I cannot lack thee two hours.

ORLANDO

I must attend the Duke at dinner, by two o'clock
I will be with thee again.   185

ROSALIND

Ay, go your ways, go your ways. I knew what
you would prove, my friends told me as much,
and I thought no less. That flattering tongue of
yours won me. 'Tis but one cast away, and so
come death. Two o'clock is your hour?   190

ORLANDO

Ay, sweet Rosalind.

ROSALIND

By my troth, and in good earnest, and so God

mend me, and by all pretty oaths that are not
dangerous, if you break one jot of your promise,
or come one minute behind your hour, I will 195
think you the most pathetical break-promise, and
the most hollow lover, and the most unworthy of
her you call Rosalind, that may be chosen out of
the gross band of the unfaithful. Therefore be-
ware my censure, and keep your promise. 200

ORLANDO

With no less religion than if thou wert indeed my
Rosalind. So adieu.

ROSALIND

Well, Time is the old justice that examines all
such offenders, and let Time try. Adieu.

[*Exit Orlando.*

CELIA

You have simply misused our sex in your love- 205
prate. We must have your doublet and hose
plucked over your head, and show the world
what the bird hath done to her own nest.

ROSALIND

O coz, coz, coz. My pretty little coz, that thou
didst know how many fathom deep I am in love. 210
But it cannot be sounded. My affection hath an
unknown bottom, like the bay of Portugal.

CELIA

Or rather bottomless, that as fast as you pour affection in, it runs out. 215

ROSALIND

No, that same wicked bastard of Venus, that was

begot of thought, conceived of spleen, and born
of madness, that blind rascally boy, that abuses
every one's eyes, because his own are out, let
him be judge how deep I am in love. I'll tell thee   220
Aliena, I cannot be out of the sight of Orlando.
I'll go find a shadow, and sigh till he come.

   CELIA
And I'll sleep.   [*Exeunt.*

Scene two

> *The forest. Enter Jaques, Lords, and
> Foresters.*

   JAQUES
Which is he that killed the deer?

   A LORD
Sir, it was I.

   JAQUES
Let's present him to the Duke like a Roman con-
queror, and it would do well to set the deer's
horns upon his head, for a branch of victory.   5
Have you no song forester for this purpose?

   FORESTER
Yes sir.

   JAQUES
Sing it: 'tis no matter how it be in tune, so it
make noise enough.   10

   ALL [*sing*]
 What shall he have that killed the deer?

His leather skin, and horns to wear.
Then sing him home. The rest shall bear
                    This burthen.
Take thou no scorn to wear the horn,
It was a crest ere thou wast born,   15
    Thy father's father wore it,
    And thy father bore it.
The horn, the horn, the lusty horn,
Is not a thing to laugh to scorn.   *[Exeunt.*

Scene three

> *The forest. Enter Rosalind and Celia.*

ROSALIND

How say you now, is it not past two a clock?
And here much Orlando!

CELIA

I warrant you, with pure love and troubled brain,
he hath ta'en his bow and arrows, and is gone
forth to sleep.

> *Enter Silvius.*

Look who comes here.   5

SILVIUS

My errand is to you, fair youth,
My gentle Phebe bid me give you this.

                          [Gives a letter.

I know not the contents, but as I guess
By the stern brow and waspish action
Which she did use as she was writing of it,   10

It bears an angry tenour; pardon me,
I am but as a guiltless messenger.

ROSALIND

Patience herself would startle at this letter,
And play the swaggerer; bear this, bear all.
She says I am not fair, that I lack manners,   15
She calls me proud, and that she could not love
    me, *bird lives 600 years - f-pyre*
Were man as rare as phœnix. 'Od's my will,
Her love is not the hare that I do hunt.
Why writes she so to me? Well shepherd, well,
This is a letter of your own device.   20

SILVIUS

No, I protest, I know not the contents,
Phebe did write it.

ROSALIND

                    Come, come, you are a fool,
And turned into the extremity of love.
I saw her hand, she has a leathern hand,
A freestone-coloured hand. I verily did think   25
That her old gloves were on, but 'twas her hands.
She has a housewife's hand, but that's no matter.
I say she never did invent this letter;
This is a man's invention, and his hand.

SILVIUS

Sure it is hers.   30

ROSALIND

Why, 'tis a boisterous and a cruel style,
A style for challengers. Why she defies me,
Like Turk to Christian. Women's gentle brain

Idleness is the Devil's workshop

Could not drop forth such giant-rude invention,
Such Ethiop words, blacker in their effect   35
Than in their countenance. Will you hear the
   letter?

> SILVIUS

So please you, for I never heard it yet.
Yet heard too much of Phebe's cruelty.

> ROSALIND

She Phebes me. Mark how the tyrant writes.
[*Reads.*] *Art thou god to shepherd turned,*   40
         That a maiden's heart hath burned?

Can a woman rail thus?

> SILVIUS

Call you this railing?

> ROSALIND [*reads*]

  Why, thy godhead laid apart,
  War'st thou with a woman's heart?   45

Did you ever hear such railing?

  Whiles the eye of man did woo me,
  That could do no vengeance to me.

Meaning me a beast.

  If the scorn of your bright eyne   50
  Have power to raise such love in mine,
  Alack, in me what strange effect
  Would they work in mild aspect?
  Whiles you chid me, I did love:
  How then might your prayers move?   55
  He that brings this love to thee,
  Little knows this love in me.
  And by him seal up thy mind,   Write back,
         seal it up

Whether that thy youth and kind
Will the faithful offer take   60
Of me, and all that I can make,
Or else by him my love deny,
And then I'll study how to die.

SILVIUS

Call you this chiding?

CELIA

Alas poor shepherd.   65

ROSALIND

Do you pity him? No, he deserves no pity. Wilt
thou love such a woman? What, to make thee an
instrument, and play false strains upon thee? Not
to be endured. Well, go your way to her, for I see
love hath made thee a tame snake, and say this to   70
her. That if she love me, I charge her to love
thee. If she will not, I will never have her, unless
thou entreat for her. If you be a true lover,
hence, and not a word, for here comes more
company.   [*Exit Silvius.*   75

Enter Oliver.   Looks for cottage

OLIVER

Good morrow, fair ones. Pray you, if you know,
Where in the purlieus of this forest stands
A sheep-cote, fenced about with olive-trees?

CELIA

West of this place, down in the neighbour bot-
    tom.
The rank of osiers, by the murmuring stream   80
Left on your right hand, brings you to the place.

But at this hour the house doth keep itself,
There's none within.

OLIVER

If that an eye may profit by a tongue,
Then should I know you by description;   85
Such garments and such years—the boy is fair,
Of female favour, and bestows himself
Like a ripe forester, the woman low,
And browner than her brother—are not you
The owner of the house I did enquire for?   90

CELIA

It is no boast, being asked, to say we are.

OLIVER

Orlando doth commend him to you both,
And to that youth he calls his Rosalind
He sends this bloody napkin. Are you he?

ROSALIND

I am. What must we understand by this?   95

OLIVER

Some of my shame, if you will know of me
What man I am, and how, and why, and where
This handkerchief was stained.

CELIA

                    I pray you tell it.

OLIVER

When last the young Orlando parted from you,
He left a promise to return again   100
Within an hour, and pacing through the forest,
Chewing the food of sweet and bitter fancy,
Lo what befell. He threw his eye aside,

And mark what object did present itself.
Under an old oak, whose boughs were mossed
   with age,   105
And high top bald with dry antiquity,
A wretched ragged man, o'ergrown with hair,
Lay sleeping on his back; about his neck
A green and gilded snake had wreathed itself,
Who with her head, nimble in threats,
   approached   110
The opening of his mouth; but suddenly,
Seeing Orlando, it unlinked itself,
And with indented glides did slip away
Into a bush, under which bush's shade
A lioness, with udders all drawn dry,   115
Lay couching head on ground, with catlike
   watch
When that the sleeping man should stir; for 'tis
The royal disposition of that beast
To prey on nothing that doth seem as dead.
This seen, Orlando did approach the man,   120
And found it was his brother, his elder brother.

     CELIA

O I have heard him speak of that same brother,
And he did render him the most unnatural
That lived amongst men.

     OLIVER

                And well he might do so,
For well I know he was unnatural.   125

     ROSALIND

But, to Orlando. Did he leave him there

Food to the sucked and hungry lioness?

OLIVER

Twice did he turn his back, and purposed so.
But kindness, nobler ever than revenge,
And nature, stronger than his just occasion, 130
Made him give battle to the lioness,
Who quickly fell before him, in which hurtling
From miserable slumber I awaked.

CELIA

Are you his brother?

ROSALIND

     Was't you he rescued?

CELIA

Was't you that did so oft contrive to kill him? 135

OLIVER

'Twas I. But 'tis not I. I do not shame
To tell you what I was, since my conversion
So sweetly tastes, being the thing I am.

ROSALIND

But for the bloody napkin?

OLIVER

     By and by.
When from the first to last betwixt us two 140
Tears our recountments had most kindly
 bathed,
As how I came into that desert place.
In brief, he led me to the gentle Duke,
Who gave me fresh array, and entertainment,
Committing me unto my brother's love, 145
Who led me instantly unto his cave,

There stripped himself, and here upon his arm
The lioness had torn some flesh away,
Which all this while had bled. And now he
    fainted,
And cried in fainting upon Rosalind.   150
Brief, I recovered him, bound up his wound,
And after some small space, being strong at
    heart,
He sent me hither, stranger as I am,
To tell this story, that you might excuse
His broken promise, and to give this napkin,   155
Dyed in his blood, unto the shepherd youth
That he in sport doth call his Rosalind.

      CELIA

Why how now Ganymede, sweet Ganymede!
                [*Rosalind faints.*

      OLIVER

Many will swoon when they do look on blood.

      CELIA

There is more in it. Cousin Ganymede!   160

      OLIVER

Look, he recovers.

      ROSALIND

I would I were at home.

      CELIA

                We'll lead you thither.
I pray you will you take him by the arm?

      OLIVER

Be of good cheer youth—you a man? You lack a
man's heart.   165

ROSALIND

I do so, I confess it. Ah, sirrah, a body would think this was well counterfeited. I pray you tell your brother how well I counterfeited. Heigh-ho!

OLIVER

This was not counterfeit, there is too great testi- 170
mony in your complexion, that it was a passion
of earnest.

ROSALIND

Counterfeit, I assure you.

OLIVER

Well then, take a good heart, and counterfeit to
be a man. 175

ROSALIND

So I do. But i' faith, I should have been a woman
by right.

CELIA

Come, you look paler and paler. Pray you draw
homewards. Good sir, go with us.

OLIVER

That will I. For I must bear answer back 180
How you excuse my brother, Rosalind.

ROSALIND

I shall devise something. But I pray you commend my counterfeiting to him. Will you go?

[*Exeunt.*

Act five Scene one

The forest. Enter Touchstone and
Audrey.

TOUCHSTONE

We shall find a time Audrey, patience gentle
Audrey.

AUDREY

Faith the priest was good enough, for all the old
gentleman's saying.

TOUCHSTONE

A most wicked Sir Oliver, Audrey, a most vile   5
Martext. But Audrey, there is a youth here in the
forest lays claim to you.

AUDREY

Ay, I know who 'tis. He hath no interest in me in
the world.

Enter William.

Here comes the man you mean.   10

TOUCHSTONE

It is meat and drink to me to see a clown. By my
troth, we that have good wits have much to answer for. We shall be flouting. We cannot hold.

WILLIAM

Good ev'n Audrey.   15

AUDREY

God ye good ev'n William.

WILLIAM

And good ev'n to you sir.

TOUCHSTONE

Good ev'n gentle friend. Cover thy head, cover
thy head. Nay prithee be covered. How old are
you friend?   20

WILLIAM

Five and twenty sir.

TOUCHSTONE

A ripe age. Is thy name William?

WILLIAM

William, sir.

TOUCHSTONE

A fair name. Wast born i' th' forest here?   25

WILLIAM

Ay sir, I thank God.

TOUCHSTONE

Thank God. A good answer. Art rich?

WILLIAM

Faith sir, so so.

TOUCHSTONE

So so is good, very good, very excellent good.
And yet it is not, it is but so so. Art thou wise?   30

WILLIAM

Ay sir, I have a pretty wit.

TOUCHSTONE

Why, thou sayst well. I do now remember a saying, the fool doth think he is wise, but the wise
man knows himself to be a fool. The heathen   35
philosopher, when he had a desire to eat a grape,
would open his lips when he put it into his
mouth, meaning thereby, that grapes were made

to eat, and lips to open. You do love this maid?   40

WILLIAM

I do sir.

TOUCHSTONE

Give me your hand. Art thou learned?

WILLIAM

No sir.   *Metaphor*

TOUCHSTONE

Then learn this of me. To have, is to have. For it
is a figure in rhetoric, that drink being poured   45
out of a cup into a glass, by filling the one doth
empty the other. For all your writers do consent
that ipse is he. Now you are not ipse, for I am he.

WILLIAM

Which he sir?   *he himself*   50

TOUCHSTONE

He sir, that must marry this woman. Therefore,
you clown, abandon—which is in the vulgar
leave—the society—which in the boorish is company—of this female—which in the common is
woman. Which together is, abandon the society   55
of this female, or clown thou perishest; or to thy
better understanding, diest; or, to wit, I kill thee,
make thee away, translate thy life into death, thy
liberty into bondage. I will deal in poison with
thee, or in bastinado, or in steel. I will bandy   60
with thee in faction. I will o'er-run thee with
policy. I will kill thee a hundred and fifty ways,
therefore tremble and depart.

AUDREY

Do good William.

WILLIAM

God rest you merry sir.   [*Exit.* 65
      Enter Corin.

CORIN

Our master and mistress seeks you. Come away,
away.

TOUCHSTONE

Trip Audrey, trip Audrey. I attend, I attend.
                                    [*Exeunt.*

Scene two

The forest. Enter Orlando and Oliver.

ORLANDO

Is't possible that on so little acquaintance you
should like her? That, but seeing, you should
love her? And loving woo? And wooing she
should grant? And will you persever to enjoy
her?   5

OLIVER

Neither call the giddiness of it in question, the
poverty of her, the small acquaintance, my sudden wooing, nor her sudden consenting. But say
with me, I love Aliena. Say with her, that she
loves me. Consent with both, that we may enjoy 10
each other. It shall be to your good. For my
father's house, and all the revenue that was old

Sir Rowland's, will I estate upon you, and here
live and die a shepherd.

ORLANDO

You have my consent. Let your wedding be to-   15
morrow. Thither will I invite the Duke, and all's
contented followers.

Enter Rosalind.

Go you and prepare Aliena, for look you, here
comes my Rosalind.

ROSALIND

God save you brother.   20

OLIVER

And you fair sister.   [*Exit.*

ROSALIND

O my dear Orlando, how it grieves me to see thee
wear thy heart in a scarf.

ORLANDO

It is my arm.

ROSALIND

I thought thy heart had been wounded with the   25
claws of a lion.

ORLANDO

Wounded it is, but with the eyes of a lady.

ROSALIND

Did your brother tell you how I counterfeited to
swoon when he showed me your handkercher?   30

ORLANDO

Ay, and greater wonders than that.

ROSALIND

O, I know where you are. Nay, 'tis true. There

was never any thing so sudden, but the fight of
two rams, and Caesar's thrasonical brag of <u>I
came, saw, and overcame</u>. For your brother, and   35
my sister, no sooner met, but they looked; no
sooner looked, but they loved; no sooner loved,
but they sighed; no sooner sighed, but they asked
one another the reason; no sooner knew the
reason, but they sought the remedy. And in these   40
degrees have they made a pair of stairs to marriage, which they will climb incontinent, or else
be incontinent before marriage; they are in the
very wrath of love, and they will together. Clubs
cannot part them.   45

    ORLANDO

They shall be married to-morrow; and I will bid
the Duke to the nuptial. But o, how <u>bitter a thing
it is to look into happiness through another</u>
man's eyes. By so much the more shall I to-
morrow be at the height of heart-heaviness, by   50
how much I shall think my brother happy in
having what he wishes for.

    ROSALIND

Why then to-morrow I cannot serve your turn
for Rosalind?

    ORLANDO

I can live no longer by thinking.   55

    ROSALIND

I will weary you then no longer with idle talking.
Know of me then—for now I speak to some purpose—that I know you are a gentleman of good

conceit. I speak not this, that you should bear a
good opinion of my knowledge, insomuch I say I　60
know you are. Neither do I labour for a greater
esteem than may in some little measure draw a
belief from you, to do yourself good, and not to
grace me. Believe then, if you please, that I can
do strange things. I have, since I was three year　65
old, conversed with a magician, most profound
in his art, and yet not damnable. If you do love
Rosalind so near the heart, as your gesture cries
it out, when your brother marries Aliena, shall
you marry her. I know into what straits of for-　70
tune she is driven; and it is not impossible to me,
if it appear not inconvenient to you, to set her
before your eyes to-morrow, human as she is,
and without any danger.　75

ORLANDO

Speak'st thou in sober meanings?

ROSALIND

By my life I do, which I tender dearly, though I
say I am a magician. Therefore put you in your
best array, bid your friends. For if you will be
married to-morrow, you shall; and to Rosalind　80
if you will.

Enter Silvius and Phebe.

Look, here comes a lover of mine, and a lover
of hers.

PHEBE

Youth, you have done me much ungentleness,
To show the letter that I writ to you.

ROSALIND

I care not if I have. It is my study   85
To seem despiteful and ungentle to you.
You are there followed by a faithful shepherd;
Look upon him, love him. He worships you.

PHEBE

Good shepherd, tell this youth what 'tis to love.

SILVIUS

It is to be all made of sighs and tears,   90
And so am I for Phebe.

PHEBE

And I for Ganymede.

ORLANDO

And I for Rosalind.

ROSALIND

And I for no woman.

SILVIUS

It is to be all made of faith and service,   95
And so am I for Phebe.

PHEBE

And I for Ganymede.

ORLANDO

And I for Rosalind.

ROSALIND

And I for no woman.

SILVIUS

It is to be all made of fantasy,   100
All made of passion, and all made of wishes,
All adoration, duty, and observance,
All humbleness, all patience, and impatience,

All purity, all trial, all observance.
And so am I for Phebe.   105

PHEBE

And so am I for Ganymede.

ORLANDO

And so am I for Rosalind.

ROSALIND

And so am I for no woman.

PHEBE [*to Rosalind*]

If this be so, why blame you me to love you?   110

SILVIUS [*to Phebe*]

If this be so, why blame you me to love you?

ORLANDO

If this be so, why blame you me to love you?

ROSALIND

Who do you speak to—why blame you me to   115
love you?

ORLANDO

To her that is not here, nor doth not hear.

ROSALIND

Pray you no more of this, 'tis like the howling of
Irish wolves against the moon. [*To Silvius.*] I
will help you if I can. [*To Phebe.*] I would love   120
you if I could.—To-morrow meet me all to-
gether.—[*To Phebe.*] I will marry you, if ever I
marry woman, and I'll be married to-morrow.
[*To Orlando.*] I will satisfy you, if ever I satis-
fied man, and you shall be married to-morrow.
[*To Silvius.*] I will content you, if what pleases   125
you contents you, and you shall be married to-

morrow. [*To Orlando.*] As you love Rosalind meet. [*To Silvius.*] As you love Phebe meet.— And as I love no woman, I'll meet. So fare you well. I have left you commands. 130

> SILVIUS

I'll not fail, if I live.

> PHEBE

Nor I.

> ORLANDO

Nor I.

[*Exeunt.*

Silvius Phoebe
Oliver Celia
Touchstone Audrey
Rosalind Orlando

Page - young errand boy

Scene three

> The forest. Enter Touchstone and
> Audrey.

> TOUCHSTONE

To-morrow is the joyful day Audrey, to-morrow will we be married.

> AUDREY

I do desire it with all my heart; and I hope it is no dishonest desire, to desire to be a woman of the world.

> *Enter two Pages.*

Here come two of the banished Duke's pages. 5

> FIRST PAGE

Well met honest gentleman.

> TOUCHSTONE

By my troth well met. Come, sit, sit, and a song.

SECOND PAGE

We are for you, sit i' th' middle.   10

FIRST PAGE

Shall we clap into't roundly, without hawking, or
spitting, or saying we are hoarse, which are the
only prologues to a bad voice?

SECOND PAGE

I' faith, i' faith, and both in a tune, like two gip-   15
sies on a horse.

PAGES [*sing*]

It was a lover, and his lass,
*   With a hey, and a ho, and a hey nonino,*
That o'er the green corn-field did pass,
*   In spring-time, the only pretty ring-time,*   2
When birds do sing, hey ding a ding, ding,
Sweet lovers love the spring.

Between the acres of the rye,
*   With a hey, and a ho, and a hey nonino,*
These pretty country-folks would lie,   2
*   In spring-time, &c.*

This carol they began that hour,
*   With a hey, and a ho, and a hey nonino,*
How that a life was but a flower,
*   In spring-time, &c.*   3

And therefore take the present time,
*   With a hey, and a ho, and a hey nonino,*
For love is crowned with the prime,
*   In spring-time, &c.*

TOUCHSTONE

Truly young gentlemen, though there was no   35
great matter in the ditty, yet the note was very
untuneable.

FIRST PAGE

You are deceived sir, we kept time, we lost not
our time.

TOUCHSTONE

By my troth yes. I count it but time lost to hear   40
such a foolish song. God b' wi' you, and God
mend your voices. Come Audrey.   [*Exeunt.*

Scene four

> *The forest. Enter Duke Senior, Amiens,*
> *Jaques, Orlando, Oliver, and Celia.*

DUKE SENIOR

Dost thou believe, Orlando, that the boy
Can do all this that he hath promised?

ORLANDO

I sometimes do believe, and sometimes do not,
As those that fear they hope, and know they
    fear.

> *Enter Rosalind, Silvius, and Phebe.*

ROSALIND

Patience once more, whiles our compact is urged   5
[*To the Duke.*] You say, if I bring in your
    Rosalind,
You will bestow her on Orlando here?

DUKE SENIOR

That would I, had I kingdoms to give with her.

ROSALIND [*to Orlando*]

And you say you will have her, when I bring her?

ORLANDO

That would I, were I of all kingdoms king.

ROSALIND [*to Phebe*]

You say, you'll marry me, if I be willing?

PHEBE

That will I, should I die the hour after.

ROSALIND

But if you do refuse to marry me,

You'll give yourself to this most faithful shepherd?

PHEBE

So is the bargain.

ROSALIND [*to Silvius*]

You say that you'll have Phebe if she will?

SILVIUS

Though to have her and death were both one
thing.

ROSALIND

I have promised to make all this matter even.

Keep you your word, o Duke, to give your
daughter,

You yours Orlando, to receive his daughter.

Keep you your word Phebe, that you'll marry
me,

Or else refusing me to wed this shepherd.

Keep your word Silvius, that you'll marry her

If she refuse me; and from hence I go,
To make these doubts all even.   25

                [Exeunt Rosalind and Celia.

    DUKE SENIOR

I do remember in this shepherd boy
Some lively touches of my daughter's favour.

    ORLANDO

My lord, the first time that I ever saw him
Methought he was a brother to your daughter.
But my good lord, this boy is forest-born,   30
And hath been tutored in the rudiments
Of many desperate studies by his uncle,
Whom he reports to be a great magician,
Obscured in the circle of this forest.

    Enter Touchstone and Audrey.

    JAQUES

There is sure another flood toward, and these   35
couples are coming to the ark. Here comes a pair
of very strange beasts, which in all tongues are
called fools.

    TOUCHSTONE

Salutation and greeting to you all.

    JAQUES

Good my lord, bid him welcome. This is the mot-   40
ley-minded gentleman that I have so often met in
the forest. He hath been a courtier he swears.

    TOUCHSTONE

If any man doubt that, let him put me to my purgation. I have trod a measure; I have flattered a   45
lady; I have been politic with my friend, smooth

with mine enemy; I have undone three tailors; I
have had four quarrels, and like to have fought
one.

JAQUES

And how was that ta'en up?   50

TOUCHSTONE

Faith we met, and found the quarrel was upon
the seventh cause.

JAQUES

How seventh cause? Good my lord, like this fellow.

DUKE SENIOR

I like him very well.   55

TOUCHSTONE

God 'ild you sir, I desire you of the like. I press
in here sir, amongst the rest of the country copulatives, to swear and to forswear, according as
marriage binds and blood breaks—a poor virgin
sir, an ill-favoured thing sir, but mine own; a   60
poor humour of mine sir, to take that that no
man else will. Rich honesty dwells like a miser
sir, in a poor house, as your pearl in your foul
oyster.

DUKE SENIOR

By my faith, he is very swift and sententious.   65

TOUCHSTONE

According to the fool's bolt sir, and such dulcet
diseases.

JAQUES

But for the seventh cause. How did you find the

quarrel on the seventh cause? *stand up straight* 70

TOUCHSTONE

Upon a lie seven times removed—bear your
body more seeming Audrey—as thus sir. I did
dislike the cut of a certain courtier's beard. He
sent me word, if I said his beard was not cut well,
he was in the mind it was. This is called the Re- 75
tort Courteous. If I sent him word again, it was
not well cut, he would send me word he cut it to
please himself. This is called the Quip Modest. If
again, it was not well cut, he disabled my judgement. This is called the Reply Churlish. If again, 80
it was not well cut, he would answer I spake not
true. This is called the Reproof Valiant. If
again, it was not well cut, he would say I lie. This
is called the Countercheck Quarrelsome; and so
to the Lie Circumstantial and the Lie Direct. 85

JAQUES

And how oft did you say his beard was not well
cut?

TOUCHSTONE

I durst go no further than the Lie Circumstantial,
nor he durst not give me the Lie Direct; and so 90
we measured swords, and parted.

JAQUES

Can you nominate in order now the degrees of
the lie?

TOUCHSTONE

O sir, we quarrel in print, by the book; as you
have books for good manners. I will name you 95

the degrees. The first, the Retort Courteous; the second, the Quip Modest; the third, the Reply Churlish; the fourth, the Reproof Valiant; the fifth, the Countercheck Quarrelsome; the sixth, the Lie with Circumstance; the seventh, the Lie Direct. All these you may avoid, but the Lie Direct. And you may avoid that too with an If. I knew when seven justices could not take up a quarrel, but when the parties were met themselves, one of them thought but of an If, as If you said so, then I said so; and they shook hands, and swore brothers. Your If is the only peacemaker. Much virtue in If.

JAQUES

Is not this a rare fellow my lord? He's as good at any thing, and yet a fool.

DUKE SENIOR

He uses his folly like a stalking-horse, and under the presentation of that he shoots his wit.

Enter Hymen and Attendants, with
Rosalind and Celia in their proper
habits. Still music.

HYMEN [*sings*]

Then is there mirth in heaven,
When earthly things made even
Atone together.
Good Duke receive thy daughter,
Hymen from heaven brought her,
Yea brought her hither,
That thou mightst join her hand with his

   Whose heart within her bosom is.
   ROSALIND [*to Duke Senior*]
To you I give myself, for I am yours.
[*To Orlando.*] To you I give myself, for I am
   yours.
      DUKE SENIOR
If there be truth in sight, you are my daughter.
      ORLANDO
If there be truth in sight, you are my Rosalind.   125
      PHEBE
If sight and shape be true,
Why then my love adieu.
      ROSALIND [*to Duke Senior*]
I'll have no father, if you be not he.
[*To Orlando.*] I'll have no husband, if you be not
   he.
[*To Phebe.*] Nor ne'er wed woman, if you be not
   she.   130
      HYMEN
   Peace ho, I bar confusion,
   'Tis I must make conclusion
      Of these most strange events.
   Here's eight that must take hands,
   To join in Hymen's bands,   135
      If truth hold true contents.
   You and you no cross shall part. *– never part*
                  [*To Orlando and Rosalind.*]
   You and you are heart in heart.
                  [*To Oliver and Celia.*]
   You to his love must accord,   [*To Phebe.*]

Or have a woman to your lord.   140

You and you are sure together,

> [*To Touchstone and Audrey.*]

As the winter to foul weather.

Whiles a wedlock-hymn we sing,

Feed yourselves with questioning.

That reason wonder may diminish   145

How thus we meet, and these things
    finish.

HYMEN *and* ATTENDANTS [*sing*]

Wedding is great Juno's crown,

  O blessed bond of board and bed.

'Tis Hymen peoples every town,

  High wedlock, then, be honoured.   150

Honour, high honour, and renown,

To Hymen, god of every town.

DUKE SENIOR

O my dear niece, welcome thou art to me,

Even daughter, welcome in no less degree.

PHEBE [*to Silvius*]

I will not eat my word, now thou art mine,   155

Thy faith my fancy to thee doth combine.

Enter Jaques de Boys.

JAQUES DE BOYS

Let me have audience for a word or two.

I am the second son of old Sir Rowland,

That bring these tidings to this fair assembly.

Duke Frederick, hearing how that every day   160

Men of great worth resorted to this forest,

Addressed a mighty power, which were on foot

In his own conduct, purposely to take
His brother here, and put him to the sword.
And to the skirts of this wild wood he came; 165
Where meeting with an old religious man,
After some question with him, was converted
Both from his enterprise, and from the world.
His crown bequeathing to his banished brother,
And all their lands restored to them again 170
That were with him exiled. This to be true,
I do engage my life.

DUKE SENIOR
           Welcome young man.
Thou offer'st fairly to thy brothers' wedding.
To one, his lands withheld, and to the other,
A land itself at large, a potent dukedom. 175
First, in this forest, let us do those ends
That here were well begun, and well begot.
And after, every of this happy number
That have endured shrewd days and nights with
    us,
Shall share the good of our returned fortune, 180
According to the measure of their states.
Meantime forget this new-fall'n dignity,
And fall into our rustic revelry.
Play, music, and you brides and bridegrooms all,
With measure heaped in joy, to th' measures fall. 185

JAQUES
Sir, by your patience. If I heard you rightly,
The Duke hath put on a religious life,
And thrown into neglect the pompous court.

JAQUES DE BOYS

He hath.

JAQUES *attend D. Fredick*

To him will I. Out of these convertites   190
There is much matter to be heard, and learned.

[*To Duke Senior.*] You to your former honour I
    bequeath;
Your patience and your virtue well deserves it.

[*To Orlando.*] You to a love that your true faith
    doth merit.

[*To Oliver.*] You to your land, and love, and
    great allies.   195

[*To Silvius.*] You to a long and well-deserved
    bed.

[*To Touchstone.*] And you to wrangling, for thy
    loving voyage *marriage — I mas.*
Is but for two months victualled. So to your
    pleasures,
I am for other than for dancing measures. *I am*

in character   DUKE SENIOR   *for other things*
Stay, Jaques, stay.   *Jack-melanch*   200

JAQUES

To see no pastime, I. What you would have,
I'll stay to know at your abandoned cave. [*Exit.*

        DUKE SENIOR

Proceed, proceed. We will begin these rites,
As we do trust they'll end in true delights.
                                [*Music and dance.*

loco – to speak

Epilogue

analogy

Backus – God of Wine

ROSALIND

It is not the fashion to see the lady the epilogue.
But it is no more unhandsome than to see the
lord the prologue. If it be true that good wine
needs no bush, 'tis true that a good play needs no
epilogue. Yet to good wine they do use good   5
bushes; and good plays prove the better by the
help of good epilogues. What a case am I in then,
that am neither a good epilogue, nor cannot in-
sinuate with you in the behalf of a good play. I
am not furnished like a beggar, therefore to beg   10
will not become me. My way is to conjure you,
and I'll begin with the women. I charge you, o
women, for the love you bear to men, to like as
much of this play as please you. And I charge
you, o men, for the love you bear to women—as   15
I perceive by your simpering, none of you hates
them—that between you and the women the play
may please. If I were a woman, I would kiss as
many of you as had beards that pleased me, com-
plexions that liked me, and breaths that I defied   20
not. And I am sure, as many as have good
beards, or good faces, or sweet breaths, will for
my kind offer, when I make curtsy, bid me farewell.
                                          [*Exeunt.*

Juy over alehouse

Shakespeare and His Theatre

BY FRANCIS FERGUSSON

I. SHAKESPEARE'S CAREER

William Shakespeare was christened in Stratford on April twenty-sixth, 1564. The exact date of his birth is unknown, but it is traditionally celebrated on the twenty-third, because that is Saint George's Day, and Saint George is England's patron saint.

The Shakespeares were a prosperous and locally prominent family. William was the oldest of six children. His father, John Shakespeare, the son of a tenant farmer, had moved to Stratford as a young man, and there built for himself a successful business career as a glover and a dealer in wool, timber, and other commodities. John also held office as Justice of the Peace and High Bailiff (Mayor); and late in life he was granted a coat of arms, which made him a "gentleman." Shakespeare's mother, Mary Arden, a member of a family of small landowners, must have brought her husband both social standing and land.

Stratford, about a hundred miles northwest of London, was a prosperous market town, one of the largest in Warwickshire. A great deal is known about Stratford, which enables us to understand something of Shakespeare's boyhood there. The town supported a grammar school which was free to the sons of Burgesses, of whom Shakespeare was one. Grammar schools were designed to prepare their students for one of the universities, and in Stratford the masters were university graduates. The education they gave was narrow but thorough. It included some history and religious instruction, but was based chiefly on Latin and the arts of language: grammar, logic, rhetoric, and what we call "public speaking." Shakespeare read a number of Latin authors, including Ovid and probably Plautus, whose comedies he imitated when he started to write for the stage. The children went to school on weekdays, summer and winter, from seven in the morning until five in the afternoon, with two hours off for dinner. Shakespeare must have started this strict routine as soon as he knew his catechism.

During his boyhood Stratford was regularly visited by touring players, including the best companies in England. The plays they brought were moralizing works on Biblical or classical themes, very wooden compared with what Shakespeare himself would write. But his future profession was highly esteemed; the players were received in the Guildhall by leading citizens, including no doubt Shakespeare's father. For the rest, we may safely imagine Shakespeare as engaged in the usual activities of a boy in a country town, acquiring the intimate knowledge of the countryside and its rural types which is reflected in his plays.

We do not know what Shakespeare did between the time he left school and his departure for London. Some of the stories about him—that he was for a time a country schoolmaster, that he got into trouble for poaching deer—are possible, but unproved. We do know that he married Ann Hathaway, daughter of a yeoman farmer, in 1582, when he was eighteen and she was twenty-three. Their first child, Susan, was baptized six months later. Perhaps the Shakespeares were "betrothed"—which, by the custom of the time, would have made them legally married—some months before the recorded church ceremony. They had two more children, the twins Hamnet and Judith, who were christened in 1585. Shakespeare departed for London very soon after that. He did not take his family with him, for he occupied bachelor's lodgings in London for most of the rest of his life. But he was also a householder in Stratford, and apparently continued to think of himself as a resident.

London, when Shakespeare went there as a young man, in about 1586, was enjoying the great years of Queen Elizabeth's reign. She had ascended the throne in 1558; in 1588 her navy had its famous victory over the Spanish Armada, which marked England's emergence as a great sea-power, and symbolized the national rebirth. The City of London had its ancient mercantile traditions, its bourgeois freedoms, and, among the City officials, a certain Puritanical spirit of its own. But the City had spread far beyond the medieval walls, and Renaissance London contained between 100,000 and 200,000 inhabitants. As the seat of Elizabeth's court it was the unrivaled center of English politics and culture. It was a university town, for the Inns of Court, resident law-schools for young gentlemen of wealth, were there; and it was full of foreigners from the continent of Europe. As a great port it was in touch with the Indies, the Mediterranean, and the Americas. Shakespeare never went to a university, but London was admirably fitted to complete his education in Italian and French, in history and literature, in the great professions, and to give him direct experience of the ways of men at an exciting moment in history. The theatre was near the center of life in Renaissance London, and Shakespeare must have been close to many of the great figures and great events of his time.

Much is known about London and about the theatres where Shakespeare worked, but little is known directly about his own doings. Contemporary comments on him, and on his plays, suggest that most of his great vitality went straight into his work for the theatre. Legal and business documents, church records, and the like, enable the experts to fix a few important dates in his personal and professional life. And the dates of his plays, though disputed in detail, are well enough established to give us the approximate sequence. It is chiefly through a study of his plays in the order in which he wrote them, and in relation to the known facts of his life, that we can gain some understanding of his development. It is convenient (following Professor Peter Alexander and others) to distinguish four main periods in Shakespeare's career:

I. Apprenticeship to the London Theatre: from Shakespeare's arrival in London (circa 1586) until he joined The Lord Chamberlain's Men, in 1594.

Shakespeare entered the theatre as an actor when he first

went to London, or as soon thereafter as he had acquired the necessary training. He was to be an actor and actor-manager for the rest of his life, and in that capacity, rather than as a playwright, he made a very good living. Playwrights received a smaller share of the theatre's revenue then than they do now. They sold their scripts outright, for very small sums, to the actors, who then divided the receipts among themselves. Shakespeare, however, began to write at once. By 1594 he had completed the following list: *Titus Andronicus; Henry VI,* Parts 1, 2, and 3; *The Comedy of Errors; Two Gentlemen of Verona; The Taming of the Shrew; Richard III; Love's Labor's Lost;* and probably *King John.*

Shakespeare's earliest work shows that he began his professional career in the most natural way: by mastering several kinds of plays that were then popular. *The Comedy of Errors, Two Gentlemen of Verona,* and *The Taming of the Shrew* are farces, based on the Latin comedy of Plautus. They have little of the poetry and subtlety of his later and more original comedies, but they are still, as they were when he wrote them, sure and effective popular entertainment. *Titus Andronicus,* a "Senecan" melodrama like other pseudo-classical plays of the time, was successful then, but usually proves too sensational and pompous for the modern stage.

The three parts of *Henry VI* are the first of Shakespeare's "Histories." The history play was a popular and characteristic form in the London theatre as Shakespeare found it. It was taken from one of the widely read Chronicles of English history, like those of Shakespeare's favorite Holinshed—a dramatization of some exciting sequence from the epic struggle of the Crown against the great nobles, the intriguing churchmen, and France and Spain. Shakespeare's generation felt that this struggle had been victoriously concluded with Elizabeth. The history plays express a somewhat jingoistic nationalism, but also, in Shakespeare's plays at least, the passion for social order and the cautious political wisdom which were making England great. *Henry VI* is the crudest of Shakespeare's Histories; it gallops, with the speed of a boy's adventure story, from one high-pitched quarrel to the next. Yet one can find in it the beginnings of some of his great and lifelong themes.

The next Histories, *Richard III* and *King John*, and the comedy, *Love's Labor's Lost*, hardly belong to Shakespeare's apprenticeship. *Love's Labor's Lost* is particularly interesting: it was written, apparently, for the Court instead of the popular audience of the public theatres. It is a gently ironic picture of an aristocratic circle infatuated with neoplatonic notions of love and learning; and it shows that Shakespeare was already at home in the "best society," and in the fashionable literary humanism of the Renaissance.

As though all this were not enough, the young Shakespeare spent part of the years 1592-94, when the Plague made one of its descents upon London and the theatres were closed, writing his narrative poems, *Venus and Adonis, The Rape of Lucrece,* and *The Phoenix and the Turtle,* and perhaps some of the sonnets too. He dedicated *Venus and Adonis* to Southampton, the famous patron of the arts. It was immediately successful, and it made Shakespeare's reputation as a writer in circles where the theatre was not considered polite literature.

I have called this period "apprenticeship," but Shakespeare began to find himself almost at once. He was born with his genius for theatrical story-telling, and also that easy sympathy with men and ideas which enabled him to share the life of his times at every point. He had, above all, the ability to learn from his own playwrighting experience. Before 1594 he was already rethinking his discoveries, thereby swiftly deepening both his vision and his art.

II. Growing Mastery: From 1594, when Shakespeare joined The Lord Chamberlain's Men, to 1599, when the Globe Theatre opened.

The Lord Chamberlain's Men, which Shakespeare joined in 1594, was the company of actor-managers with whom he was to work for the rest of his life. It was the best company in London, including Richard Burbage, soon to be recognized as England's leading actor; Heminge and Condell, who were to publish the First Folio of Shakespeare's plays after his death; and Will Kempe, the renowned comedian. Their patron, the Lord Chamberlain (Lord Hunsdon) was a member of the Queen's Privy Council, in charge of her household and all the entertainments. He did not support his players; their income came mostly from their large public audiences. But he lent them the prestige of the Crown, defended them from the officials of the City of London (who had a bourgeois and puritanical mistrust of the theatre), and arranged for their frequent and well-paid appearances at Court. In addition to regular performances in the public theatres and at Court, The Lord Chamberlain's Men toured the provinces in the summer, and sometimes at other seasons also, when the Plague forced the closing of the City theatres.

In 1595 Shakespeare's only son, Hamnet, died in Stratford at the age of eleven. In 1597 he bought New Place, the largest house in Stratford, evidence that he was making a good living, and also that he continued to think of himself as a resident of his native town.

He wrote the following plays in approximately this period: *Romeo and Juliet; Richard II; Henry IV,* Parts I and 2; *The Merchant of Venice; A Midsummer Night's Dream; The Merry Wives of Windsor; Much Ado about Nothing; Henry V; As You Like It;* and perhaps *Twelfth Night.*

These are the plays of the most popular playwright of the day: Shakespeare was giving his public what it wanted. But he was also unfolding, through the popular tales he dramatized, his own intimate sense of human life. The plays may be classified as Comedies, Histories, and Tragedies, but each one is unique. They owe more to Shakespeare's own flexible art than they do to the theatrical conventions he inherited.

Richard II and *Henry IV,* Parts 1 and 2, are freer and deeper in language, in their rather disillusioned political wisdom, and above all in their character-drawing, than the early Histories. By the time he wrote *Henry V* Shakespeare seems to have tired of the History play, tied as it was to familiar events and to the immediate issues of politics. In the next phase he will turn from literal history to the freer and deeper form of tragedy.

The comedies of this period, the "Golden Comedies," are far more original in form and spirit than the "plotty" Latin farces of his apprenticeship. The titles and subtitles (*As You Like It*, or *Twelfth Night, Or What You Will*, for instance) suggest that Shakespeare was meeting a public demand for more plays like *A Midsummer Night's Dream*. But at the same time he was exploring an inspiration of his own. He had learned to combine several stories of different kinds in such a way as to suggest, in each play, a single poetic and ruefully smiling vision of human life. He presents the delusions of youth as fond and charming; he stages them in the light of dream, or of some brief festive occasion. The only exception is *The Merry Wives*, a farce which he may have written at the Queen's request.

The Merchant of Venice and *Romeo and Juliet* are akin in spirit to the comedies, but each represents also a new discovery. *The Merchant* is Shakespeare's first serious play about a commercial republic, and his first ambitious experiment in allegory. *Romeo and Juliet* brings into the theatre, for the first time, the themes, the music, and even the verse-forms of a very old tradition in European love-poetry, and in its structure foreshadows the great tragedies of the next phase.

In these intense five years Shakespeare's genius was coming into its own, and one can see its growth in every aspect of his complex art. His fabulous gift is most evident, perhaps, in the great characters that suddenly people his stage. Harry and Falstaff in *Henry IV*, Shylock in *The Merchant*, the Nurse in *Romeo*, Beatrice and Benedick in *Much Ado*, must have surprised even their author. One can see that Shakespeare's imagination was fed by the lively types that swarmed around him in London, and also by the actors whom he knew so well in his own company. A working theatre is a small society in itself, analogous to the larger human world around it. One can often feel, in the many-sided humanity of Shakespeare's characters—their fatness or leanness, their tricks of speech, life-rhythms that express certain temperaments—the presence of flesh-and-blood actors who would perform them. Perhaps Shakespeare's creations owe as much to his acting-company as to the stories he used. Yet in the long run they live with the life of Shakespeare's poetic imagination, which is more intense than any direct mimicry could be.

> *III. Maturity: The years of the great tragedies, from the acquisition of the Globe Theatre in 1599 to the acquisition of the Blackfriars' Theatre in 1608.*

In 1599 The Lord Chamberlain's Men acquired the illustrious Globe Theatre, which they were to occupy for the rest of Shakespeare's life. Elizabeth died in 1603, and James I ascended the throne. Fortunately James was as fond of the theatre as Elizabeth had been. He made The Lord Chamberlain's Men "The King's Men," thus taking Shakespeare's company under his royal patronage, and recognizing it as the finest in London. The King's Men seem to have enjoyed almost unbroken success, for they played often at Court and continued to attract large audiences at the Globe.

Shakespeare wrote the following plays in this period of eight or nine years: *Julius Caesar; Hamlet; All's Well that Ends Well; Troilus and Cressida; Measure for Measure; Othello; King Lear; Macbeth; Antony and Cleopatra; Timon of Athens; Coriolanus.*

The list looks to succeeding generations like a unique but natural miracle, a Sequoia Forest of the human spirit. No one has succeeded in mapping it satisfactorily, and every new reader is free to enjoy and explore it as his own understanding slowly grows.

Many attempts have been made to "explain" Shakespeare's tragic phase as the result of circumstances in his own life. We know that Hamnet, his only son, died in 1596, his father in 1601, and his mother in 1608. The last years of Queen Elizabeth's reign were darkened by trouble at home and abroad, especially her long quarrel with Essex. James's reign too, after a brief period of hopefulness, was filled with the beginnings of disorder. All over Europe the end of the Renaissance was a time of confusion and frightening premonitions of change. All of this, and probably more intimate experiences of which we know nothing, must have been grist to Shakespeare's mill. But the crucial question, how experience is transmuted into tragic poetry, is unanswerable.

The most illuminating studies are based on the plays themselves, and their relationships to earlier work, for Shakespeare (like other great artists) learned continually by rethinking his own achievements. It has been pointed out that some of the tragic characters grew, by mysterious processes of transformation and combination, out of their predecessors: Hamlet from Richard II, Brutus, Romeo; Macbeth from Richard III, perhaps Bolingbroke in *Richard II* and *Henry IV*. Shakespeare's mature mastery of versification, and also of form and plot, were the outcome of long practice; the musical harmony of imagery and symbol in a late play like *Antony and Cleopatra* was the fruit of years of writing. About the turn of the century the varied elements fell into place, and Shakespeare began to enjoy his full mastery.

The tragedies proper, especially *Hamlet, King Lear,* and *Macbeth,* which have to do with the tragic paradoxes of kingship, may be thought of as deeper mutations of the Histories. Like the Histories, these three plays picture the kind of society that Shakespeare knew and loved best, that of the Tudor monarchy. But Hamlet's Denmark, Lear's ancient Britain, and Macbeth's Scotland are not literally contemporary England. The stories of those plays are not, like the Histories, connected with familiar political struggles. Intimate as they are in detail, immediate though their life is—and instantly convincing—they have at the same time a certain legendary distance. They are mirrors in which Shakespeare could freely reflect the universal meanings he had found in his own and his country's experience.

The Roman tragedies, *Julius Caesar* and *Coriolanus,* are also derived from the Histories, but the Roman setting gives them a different quality. The characters and many details

in these plays are Tudor English, but there is no doubt that
Shakespeare wished them to evoke ancient Rome. Rome
and its history had haunted the imagination of Europe since
the dark ages, and Shakespeare's imagination since his
schooldays; but he did not love Rome as he loved (and
sometimes despaired of) his own monarchical society. He
sees the fate of a Brutus or a Coriolanus in a colder and
harder human world; between the mob one way and the
wise but helpless philosophy of a Menenius, or the ration-
alizations of Brutus himself, the other way. In short, Rome,
or the legendary idea of Rome, gave him another mirror in
which to reflect another aspect of his tragic vision. And
Othello reflects it in still another context. Set (like *The
Merchant of Venice* and *Timon of Athens*) in a commercial
republic, it is Shakespeare's most modern or "domestic"
tragedy, foreshadowing Ibsen's well-made drama of indi-
vidualism.

Even if one thinks only of the plays properly called
"Tragedies," one can see that Shakespeare's sense of human destiny had not only deepened but widened, and now
included most of the forms of human life and society visible at that time, the threshold of the modern world. But
what are we to say of the other plays in the list? *Antony
and Cleopatra,* for all its mortal sadness, hardly feels
"tragic"; it floats like a dream, a transfiguration of the
Golden Comedies. *Measure for Measure,* akin both to *Hamlet* and *The Tempest,* is a self-conscious political and theo-
logical allegory. *Troilus and Cressida,* conceived perhaps
as a gigantic farce, has come to seem, since the early 'thir-
ties, a prophetic picture of our own faithless "wars and
lecheries." And so on. We cannot hope to grasp all of the
aspects of Shakespeare's vision as it unfolded in these years,
to say nothing of holding them all together.

But we can safely say that, just as the facts show that he
was enjoying brilliant professional success, so the plays
show "success" in a more intimate sense. The human creature must have appeared to him in an appalling light: "We
that are young/ Shall never see so much, or live so long."
But when we read the plays and hear their music, we are

reminded that the tragic emotion includes exaltation. To
have faced and then projected the tragic vision in poetry
was a triumph of spirit. Shakespeare completed the great
labors of his maturity in undiminished strength. Then he
went on to digest the tragic vision in its turn, placing it in
the serener perspective of the end of his life in the theatre.

*IV. Synthesis and Serenity: From the acquisition of
the Blackfriars' Theatre in 1608 to Shakespeare's death
in Stratford in 1616.*

The King's Men bought the Blackfriars' Theatre in 1608,
and thereafter used it regularly, in bad weather, in addition
to their Globe Theatre. Blackfriars' was so called because
it was in one of the monasteries which had been taken over
by the Crown under Henry VIII. It was an indoor theatre,
and had been used for some years by a company of boy-
actors. The influence of its indoor stage can be seen in
Shakespeare's last plays; and the increasing use of indoor
stages from this time onward prepared the evolution of
the modern theatre. The "Inn-yard theatres," like the Globe,
for which most of Shakespeare's plays were written, were
soon to disappear.

The purchase of Blackfriars' is one of several signs that
Shakespeare was ending his theatrical career in comfort and
prosperity. Some time after 1610 he began, probably gradu-
ally, to retire from active work in the theatre, and his last
days were spent in his house, New Place, in Stratford. His
bequests, including the famous one of his "second-best bed"
to his wife, reveal a very substantial citizen of his native
town. His small legacies to fellow members of The King's
Men show his respect and affection for his lifelong colleagues; and the preface which Heminge and Condell wrote
for their First Folio of his plays shows that they continued
to revere him eight years after his death. Shakespeare's
company must have possessed some rare virtues in addition
to their talent, for The King's Men lasted longer than any
theatre group in the English-speaking world, before or since.
And Shakespeare's art owes a great deal to the acting ensemble for which he wrote.

He completed the following plays in this period: *Pericles; Cymbeline; The Winter's Tale; The Tempest;* and *Henry VIII*.

Henry VIII completes Shakespeare's chronicle of English history with the auspicious birth of Elizabeth, but it is a pageant and an allegory, rather than a History like the earlier plays which are so called. It is more interesting to the modern reader for the indirect light it sheds on Shakespeare's politics than as a play in its own right.

The other four plays, which were written in the order in which they are listed above, represent the harmonious end of Shakespeare's career. They are not tragedies, but theatre-poetry with subtle and manifold allegorical meanings. Each of their stories covers a whole generation, from childhood to age, instead of a single profound crisis like the stories of the tragedies. They are full of echoes of the earlier themes, as though Shakespeare were looking back over the course of his life and art. *The Tempest* is the last, the richest, and the most assured masterpiece of the four. Miranda and Ferdinand give us again the music of youth and its brave new world; the usurping Duke, with his treacheries, reminds us of the themes of guilt and suffering in the Histories and Tragedies. All these figures—and Caliban and Ariel and Gonzago and the rest—are lovingly brooded over by the Magician, Prospero, now ready to renounce the glorious cares of art and rule. It is natural to see Prospero as an image of Shakespeare, and the play as his own last word on the form and meaning of his own career, a detached but moving reflection of life from the cradle to the grave. Such a reading confirms the impression one gets from the sequence of Shakespeare's plays, and from the known facts of his life: that, more than any other man, he knew and gratefully accepted the mysterious experience of everyman.

Shakespeare did not impress his contemporaries as a spectacular personality, though many of them knew he was the foremost dramatist of that, or perhaps any, age. Ben Jonson, in the verses he wrote to go with the portrait in the First Folio, speaks for all who attempt to picture Shakespeare:

To the Reader.

This Figure, that thou here seest put,
  It was for gentle Shakespeare cut:
Wherein the Graver had a strife
  with Nature, to out doo the life:
O, could he but have drawne his wit
  As well in brasse, as he hath hit
His face, the Print would then surpasse
  All, that was ever writ in brasse.
But, since he cannot, Reader, looke
  Not on his Picture, but his Booke.

Shakespeare died in Stratford in 1616, at the unbelievably early age of fifty-two.

II. SHAKESPEARE'S THEATRE

Shakespeare wrote most of his plays for the Globe Theatre. He wrote also for the Court, the Inns of Court, and, toward the end of his career, for the indoor stage of the Black-friars' Theatre. But it was the Globe, its permanent acting-company, and its large public audiences, which chiefly de-termined the style of Shakespeare's dramaturgy. That thea-tre was Shakespeare's instrument, as important for his art as the orchestra available to a composer is for the music he writes.

Most of our knowledge of the Globe is derived from the contemporary sketch of the Swan—like the Globe, one of the "public theatres"—which is reproduced on the second page following. Recent students of Shakespeare's theatre have made far more elaborate, and largely conjectural, reconstruc-tions of the Globe. (For three of the most valuable studies, see "Suggestions for Further Reading," below.) The follow-ing simplified description refers to the accompanying sketch.

In the center, the stage-house, where the actors dressed and stored their costumes and properties, rises to a height of three stories, and is topped by the "hut," where the flag flies. In front of it the platform (five or six feet above the ground) projects into the "yard" where the groundlings stood. The yard is encircled by three roofed balconies, and there the richer members of the audience sat on cushioned seats. The yard and part of the platform are open to the sky. The façade of the stage-house has large double doors on either side, and the Globe had also a central opening (not shown in the sketch) equipped with curtains which could be closed, or opened to reveal an inner room. There is a large balcony at the second-story level; and the hut could be used for musicians, sound effects, and machinery. A roof, called "the heavens," supported on tall, ornate pillars, covers the upper stage; and there was a trapdoor in the platform leading down to the cellar or "hell," which could also be entered from inside the stage-house.

This theatre may strike us as primitive, but Shakespeare's contemporaries thought it rich and splendid. The interior was elaborately carved and painted, in a style like that of the allegorical archways erected in the London streets for James the First's coronation. For performances the stage would be hung with banners and tapestries, or, for a tragedy, with black. The actors were gorgeously and expensively costumed, and they used elaborate properties, not only "hand-props" like weapons and torches, but portable thrones, altars, and the like. They made frequent use of sound effects for thunder or the noise of battle. Music, a widely cultivated art at the time, was important. In Shakespeare's plays it was an essential element of his theatrical "orchestration." He used it to change the mood, to stress a rhythm, or to punctuate the movement of the story.

The stage of the Globe, complicated as it was, was a permanent· setting entirely unlike the modern "picture-frame" stage. Realistic or illusory settings of the kind we know were impossible, and the permanently visible structure could not be changed. The light came from the sky, and the resources of modern lighting were undreamed of. The effect was to focus attention upon the actors and what they said. The Globe could accommodate two thousand spectators or more, but packed closely around three sides of the stage, they could follow the subtleties of the playing

The Swan Theatre. Based on a drawing by Johannes de Witt in Arend van Buchell's commonplace book.

like audiences in our "arena" theatres. The audience looked, perforce, to the actors, not only to create the characters, but also to build imaginatively, in word and deed, the changing scenes of the story.

There is every reason to believe that the actors in Shakespeare's company were up to their great task. The arts of language both written and spoken were carefully culitivated, in the schools and pulpits as well as in the theatre. Actors were expected not only to command the language, but to dance, sing, play musical instruments, and fence well enough to please the connoisseurs. Women's parts were taken by boys, also highly trained. They had often been choristers, accustomed to singing good and difficult music, or members of one of the children's theatres. According to some contemporary testimony, they were better than the actresses on the continent. The art of acting, indeed—as distinguished from type-casting or the exploitation of the actor's sex or personality—was apparently well understood. The actors were used to playing a great variety of roles, often several parts in one production. The great Burbage played such varied characters as Hamlet, Macbeth, and Othello. Shakespeare himself must have chosen him for these roles, or written the roles for him, which strongly suggests that he was an artist with a very flexible and reliable technique. Shakespeare himself was an actor, and the art of acting is at the very root of his whole playwrighting art. We must think of that company, not like the cast of a Broadway show, hastily assembled for four weeks' rehearsal, but as resembling one of the highly trained companies of modern Europe. It must have been, in short, an accomplished and experienced ensemble.

Shakespeare's unrealistic or make-believe theatre, with the skilled player on the nearly empty platform, gave the dramatic poet great imaginative freedom. Modern playwrights often envy this freedom, and seek it on the arenastage or on the bare stage. Thornton Wilder's *Our Town*, for instance, counts entirely on the actors and the willing audience to establish the scenes of the play. But Shakespeare's theatre, in its very structure, placed the poet and actors in the center, and so determined the style we know. In the opening scene of *Hamlet* Shakespeare, with the aid of two players, creates the night on the parapet in a matter of seconds:

> BARNARDO: 'Tis now struck twelve, get thee to bed Francisco.
>
> FRANCISCO: For this relief much thanks, 'tis bitter cold, And I am sick at heart.
>
> BARNARDO: Have you had quiet guard?
>
> FRANCISCO: Not a mouse stirring.

Much of the sweep of Shakespeare's poetry, its power to evoke scenes of many kinds and moods, is based on the collaboration between poet, actor, and audience in a theatre where literal realism was impossible.

On that stage, moreover, Shakespeare was not limited to a realistic time-scheme, or to detailed specifications of place. He used both time and place, not for documentation, but as means of conveying the action of the story. It is a mistake to inquire (as many students have felt obliged to do) just how many days or weeks Hamlet spent in England, or just which room in the palace Cleopatra occupies at the moment; such information is irrelevant to the unfolding of the play.

The stage of the Globe was, however, an extremely flexible instrument for suggesting changes of place where that was essential. The main playing-area was no doubt the platform, but the stage-house façade offered many other possibilities for the make-believe of the players. The big doors could be opened for the entrance of military processions, funerals, or royal progresses. The balcony could represent a castle-parapet, or Cleopatra's monument, or Juliet's bedroom window. The central opening might be used as an inner room, or its curtains might be suddenly opened to reveal a special effect, a prepared "set-piece" like the armed head, bloody child, and endless row of kings with which the Witches startle Macbeth. Careful studies of recent years have shown us how flexible that stage was. The clarity and theatrical effectiveness of Shakespeare's plays is evident as soon as one understands the stage for which he wrote them.

The traditional divisions of Shakespeare's plays into acts and scenes, with indications of place for every scene, were added by the long sequence of editors of the texts. The plays were originally played straight through, with no intermissions, and with only such suggestions of place as emerged from the play itself. The traditional labels of act, scene, and place are retained in this series to assist the reader (who does not have the benefit of Shakespeare's stage) to get his bearings. But to sense the rhythm which Shakespeare intended, one should think of the play as unfolding without a break from beginning to end.

One should also know something about what the theatre meant to Shakespeare's Londoners, for a theatre is partly the creation of its audience. The theatre was the Londoner's chief form of amusement, rivaled only by the bawdy-houses and the savage sport of bear-baiting. Everyone went to the theatre: the much-maligned groundlings who could stand in the yard and watch the show for a penny; law students, by all accounts a lively and intelligent group; the nobles and rich merchants, with their ladies; the " 'prentices," who have been described as clerks and young business people; in short, a cross-section of that great generation. They did not have our newspapers, magazines, movies, radio or television. Even books were much rarer and harder to get than they are now. The London theatre was a chief medium of public communication and an important instrument in the building of the common picture of man and his society. Holinshed and other recent Chroniclers were interpreting English history as leading up to Elizabeth's beloved reign; Roman history, Italian and French fiction, and old stories and legends of many kinds, were widely read; and narratives from all these sources were made to live again in the performances of the players. Hamlet must have expressed the common feeling when he called the players "abstracts and brief chronicles of the time." His definition of the purpose of playing suggests what the theatre meant then: "To hold, as 'twere, the mirror up to nature; to show virtue her own feature, scorn her own image, and the very age and body of the time his form and pressure."

The proud device which Shakespeare's company adopted for their Globe Theatre was Hercules lifting the sphere of the earth. There are many indications in Shakespeare's plays that he thought of his theatre's "wooden O" as a microcosm, a symbolic representation of man's world as that age conceived it. Burbage, playing Hamlet, could point to the platform on which he stood as "this goodly frame, the earth," which seemed to him, in his melancholy, "a sterile premontory." When he spoke of the heavens as "this majestical roof fretted with golden fire" he had the actual roof far above his head, which was in fact painted, probably with stars, signs of the zodiac, or allegorical figures. When he heard his father's ghost the sound came from the cellerage or "hell" under the platform. Thus Shakespeare used his stage, not only to present the immediate events of the story, but also the cosmic setting where man, crawling between heaven and earth, met his mysterious fate. The modern reader can enter the world of Shakespeare's poetry more easily, and with fuller understanding, if he remembers that the symbolic stage itself was a basis for it.

III. SHAKESPEARE ON THE MODERN STAGE

The Puritan Revolution put an end to the theatre as Shakespeare had known it in 1642, when Parliament prohibited all stage-plays. The Restoration reopened the theatres in 1660, but the players had moved indoors, and most of the public theatres that Shakespeare used were gone. D'Avenant and Killigrew revived Shakespeare's plays at once, but Shakespeare would hardly have recognized them. The understanding of his art had decayed along with the theatres in which it was formed.

D'Avenant began the practice of adapting and "improving" Shakespeare for the new theatre. He arranged the plays for the indoor stages of Restoration London, which were already beginning to resemble our proscenium-stages, dividing them into scenes which could be realistically or spectacularly set. He also drastically altered the texts to suit the taste of the new society. He cut or re-wrote passages which he found indelicate; he re-arranged plots to make them "clearer" or more moral; and he was quite willing to shift whole scenes from one play to another. Many of his bad habits governed the staging of Shakespeare almost to our own day. The barnstorming Shakespeareans whom our grandfathers saw in opera-houses all over this country were essentially within that tradition.

It was Granville-Barker, after William Poel, who did the most to free the staging of Shakespeare from its inherited encumbrances. He demonstrated in his own productions and in his famous *Prefaces to Shakespeare* that the plays—including those which had been thought literary and un-stageable—are extraordinarily clear and effective in the theatre, provided the director does not feel obliged to pause and set a realistic scene with every change of place. As the implications of Granville-Barker's views were worked out, the flexibility and imaginative scope of Shakespeare's stage-techniques became clearer and clearer to a new generation in the theatre.

Contemporary producers inherit this improved under-standing of Shakespeare's purely theatrical effectiveness. There is no longer any need to think that Shakespeare is hard to stage simply because realistic staging strangles him. Moreover our theatre is no longer limited to realism or heavy romantic spectacle. We are accustomed to perma-nent settings, arenas, bare stages, and other arrangements designed to secure for poet and performer the kind of freedom Shakespeare enjoyed. The modern producer is in a good position to understand Shakespeare's theatrical in-tentions, and he is free, after that, to consult his own taste —subject, of course, to the limitations imposed by his budget, his actors, and his audience.

If no standard form of Shakespeare-staging has emerged in our time, that is because the theatre itself is so varied. The productions we see, good and bad in different ways, reflect a bewildering variety of intentions. Modern dress

may be used to stress the contemporaneity of a play like
Troilus; productions like Copeau's use period music and
costume for poetic purposes; *Coriolanus* or *Julius Caesar*
may be pointed up in such a way as to bring out a fascist
(or anti-fascist) thesis. Shakespeare is constantly adapted
to the movies, television, radio, and dance and opera. In
recent years off-Broadway, college, and community theatres
have often staged Shakespeare "straight"—relying on the
acting and directing, and spending very little on sets and
costumes. Some of these productions have had great vitality and unexpected but convincing subtlety; probably they
give the best sense of Shakespeare's own direct theatrical
style.

There is room in our time for many interpretations of
Shakespeare, both on and off the stage. The comments on
separate plays in this series, written by well-known actors,
directors, poets, and critics, are intended to suggest some of
the living approaches to Shakespeare, and some of the
meanings which his many-sided art has for us.

SUGGESTIONS FOR FURTHER READING

This short list is intended to assist the reader who wishes to
inform himself further about Shakespeare in the light of
modern studies. Most of the books referred to are easy to
find in libraries or recent editions. Asterisks (*) indicate
books available in paperbound editions.

Many of the books listed below contain bibliographies,
and more detailed studies of particular plays are listed in
the Introductions to this series.

I. SHAKESPEARE'S LIFE AND TIMES

*Chute, Marchette. *Shakespeare of London.* New York:
1956.

An excellent popular biography, containing the known
facts without the usual uncertain speculations. Espe-

cially valuable for its careful accounts of Stratford, London, Shakespeare's theatres, and his colleagues and patrons.

Halliday, F. E. *Shakespeare: A Pictorial Biography*. New York: 1956.

A short account of the known facts of Shakespeare's life and surroundings, profusely illustrated with photographs, prints, and other pictorial materials.

*Trevelyan, G. M. *History of England*. Volume II: The Tudors and the Stuart Era. New York: 1953.

A short and readable account of English history in the time of Shakespeare.

Tillyard, E. M. W. *The Elizabethan World Picture*. New York: 1944.

A description of the way man, his society, and his world looked in Shakespeare's time. It throws light on Shakespeare's theatre, which was a kind of model of the Elizabethan's "world," and on the background of his poetry.

*Fluchère, Henri. *Shakespeare and the Elizabethans*, with a Foreword by T. S. Eliot. New York: 1956.

A recent and stimulating book on Shakespeare the dramatist, in relation to other Elizabethans, and to the times in which they lived.

*Eliot, T. S. *Essays on Elizabethan Drama*. New York: 1956.

Brief essays which do not include Shakespeare, but the book is one of the most influential of recent years, and clearly illustrates the new interest in the poetry and drama of Shakespeare's age.

II. SHAKESPEARE IN THE THEATRE

Adams, John Cranford. *The Globe Playhouse: Its Design and Equipment*. New York: 1942.

Hodges, C. Walter. *The Globe Restored*. New York: 1954.

Smith, Irwin. *Shakespeare's Globe Playhouse. A Modern Reconstruction in Text and Scale Drawings*. New York: 1956.

> Dr. Adams's book is the most elaborate recent effort to reconstruct Shakespeare's own theatre. It is based on painstaking scholarship, but many details are necessarily conjectural, and are questioned by other authorities. The other two books rely very much on Dr. Adams's, but differ in details. Mr. Smith is interested in the methods of actual construction in Shakespeare's time. Mr. Hodges' study is the shortest and most readable, and contains many well-chosen illustrations.

Granville-Barker, Harley. *Prefaces to Shakespeare*. Princeton: 1946.

> The fundamental book on Shakespeare's plays as works for the theatre. Ten plays are discussed from the point of view of their staging as Shakespeare himself planned it. Granville-Barker was both an authority on Shakespeare's stage and a skilled director in the modern theatre.

De Banke, Cecile. *Shakespearean Production, Then and Now. A Manual for the Scholar Player*. New York: 1953.

Watkins, Ronald. *On Producing Shakespeare*. London: 1950.

*Webster, Margaret. *Shakespeare without Tears*. New York: 1957.

> These three books are concerned with the modern staging of Shakespeare. Professor De Banke's is addressed primarily to the school or college director. Mr. Watkins is talking to professionals, and arguing for the necessity of understanding Shakespeare's own theatre-practice. Miss Webster speaks out of her wide experience as a producer of Shakespeare here and in England. Her book is useful also for those who wish only to read the plays.

III. CRITICISM AND INTERPRETATION

Bradley, A. C. Shakespearean Tragedy. New York: 1955
Bradley summarizes the best nineteenth century criticism, which emphasizes the creation of character. His book is one of the foundations for the modern understanding of Shakespeare. This volume is concerned primarily with *Hamlet, Othello, King Lear,* and *Macbeth.*

Goddard, Harold C. *The Meaning of Shakespeare.* Chicago: 1950.
A stimulating reading of all of Shakespeare; a useful and provocative introduction.

*Traversi, D. A. *An Approach to Shakespeare.* New York: 1956.
A short study by a well-known English critic who has taken account of recent developments in Shakespeare criticism.

*Van Doren, Mark. *Shakespeare.* New York: 1953.
A reading of all of Shakespeare's works by a scholar who is also a sensitive lyric poet.

Clemen, W. H. *The Development of Shakespeare's Imagery.* Cambridge, Mass.: 1951.

Moulton, R. G. *Shakespeare as Dramatic Artist.* Oxford: 1929.

These two books, which are somewhat technical, are concerned with Shakespeare's art as a writer of plays. Clemen's book may serve as an introduction to the many recent studies of Shakespeare's poetry. Moulton's is still the best analysis of Shakespeare's methods in constructing his plots.

Shakespeare Criticism: A Selection. Smith, D. N. editor. Oxford: 1916.

Shakespeare Criticism, 1919-1935. Selected with an Introduction by Anne Bradby. Oxford: 1936.

**Shakespeare. Modern Essays in Criticism*. Dean, Leonard F., editor. New York: 1957.

> These three books constitute a useful sampling of the vast literature of Shakespeare criticism from his own time to ours.

IV. REFERENCE BOOKS

The New Variorum Shakespeare. H. H. Furness and H. H. Furness, editors. Philadelphia: 1878–.

> Most of Shakespeare's more important plays have appeared in this series, which is being continued by a committee of the Modern Language Association. It contains exhaustive notes on textual problems, many critical comments, and some sources.

The First Folio of Shakespeare's Plays, in a Facsimile Edition. Helge Kokeritz and Charles Tyler Prouty, editors. New Haven: 1955.

> The facsimile of the First Folio, published originally by Shakespeare's colleagues, is harder to read than a modern edition; but the old spelling and punctuation give valuable insights into Shakespeare's language.

C. J. Sisson. *New Readings in Shakespeare*. Two Vols. Cambridge: 1956.

> The latest authoritative survey of the problems of Shakespeare's text, with an illuminating essay on modern methods of textual analysis, by the textual editor of this series.

A Shakespeare Glossary. C. T. Onions, editor. Oxford: 1919.

A New and Complete Concordance or Verbal Index to Words, Phrases, and Passages in the Dramatic Works of Shakespeare. John Bartlett, compiler. New York: 1894.

Chambers, E. K. *The Elizabethan Stage*. Four Vols. Oxford: 1923.

Chambers, E. K. *William Shakespeare: A Study of Facts and Problems*. Oxford: 1930.

> The two works of Chambers are a mine of information, and the foundation of a great deal of modern Shakespeare scholarship.

Bentley, G. E. *The Jacobean and Caroline Stage*. Five Vols. Oxford: 1941-56.
> This is the standard work on the English stage. It carries Chambers' work, which ends with the death of Shakespeare, to the closing of the theatres. Volumes I and II are devoted to "Dramatic Companies and Players," Volumes III, IV, and V to "Plays and Playwrights."

Shakespeare's England: An Account of the Life and Manners of His Age. Two Vols. Oxford: 1916.
> A collection of essays by experts in various fields, planned by the late Sir Walter Raleigh. Very useful as background for the plays.

Ralli, Augustus. *A History of Shakespeare Criticism*. Two Vols. Oxford: 1932.

Odell, George C. D. *Shakespeare from Betterton to Irving*. Two Vols. New York: 1920.
> A history of Shakespeare productions since the Restoration.

A Companion to Shakespeare Studies. Granville-Barker, Harley, and Harrison, G. B., editors. New York: 1934.
> Essays by leading authorities on Shakespeare's life, theatre, poetry, and sources, and on scholarly and critical problems. Useful in itself and as a guide to further study.

Ebisch, Walther, and Schucking, L. L. *A Shakespeare Bibliography*. Oxford: 1931.
——— Supplement for the Years 1930-1935. Oxford: 1937.

Glossary Notes

This glossary, based on the glossary prepared for Hilda Hulme for the *Complete Works of Shakespeare*, edited by C. J. Sisson, was made especially for *As You Like It* by H. H. Smith. Unfamiliar words, foreign phrases, mythological allusions, and English words used in unfamiliar senses are defined here. Words which may easily be found in any standard modern dictionary are generally not included.

Adam: see *penalty of Adam*.

adventure: accident, chance.

affections: passions, feelings.

against: in expectation of.

Aliena: the estranged, the cast off (from Latin).

allottery: portion, share.

an: if.

anatomize: to dissect, expose in detail.

and if: if only.

anon: soon, presently.

argument: cause, subject-matter.

Atalanta: mythological heroine who challenged her suitors to a foot-race, death being the penalty for defeat and her hand the reward for outrunning her. Hippomenes defeated her by dropping three golden apples which she stopped to pick up. "Atalanta's better part," then, is her swiftness rather than her greed.

atomies: motes, specks of dust.

atone: to unite, reconcile, to make "at one."

bandy: to contend, fight.

Barbary: country on the north coast of Africa.

bastard of Venus: Cupid, the illegitimate child of Venus and Mars.

bastinado: beating, cudgeling.

batlet: a wooden instrument used for beating clothes while washing them.

bawd: pimp.

bawdry: illicit intercourse.

bell-wether: the leading sheep of a flock which wears a bell.

bill: notice, label, advertisement.

blow: to deposit eggs on, to make foul (in addition to the obvious meaning).

blue eye: an eye with dark circles from sleeplessness.

bob: to trick, taunt.

bolt: broad-headed arrow.

bonjour: good day.

bow: yoke.

bravery: finery, splendor, ostentation.

brawl: to make noise.

breathed: exercised.

broken music: music in parts, arranged for different instruments; with a pun on the breaking of the ribs of a musical instrument.

brook: to tolerate, endure.

buckle in: to limit.

bugle: black bead.

burthen: refrain, burden.

bush: an ivy bush (sacred to Bacchus, the god of wine) was the sign of a vintner.

butter women's rank: a line of women jogging to market to sell their butter.

calling: name.

capable: able to receive or be affected by.

capricious: Touchstone is punning on the Latin "caper" meaning "he-goat." The pun is continued in "Goths," probably pronounced "goats" in Elizabethan English. The goat is a traditional symbol of lust, hence the inclusion of Ovid.

carlot: peasant.

carol: festival song.

cart: to punish a whore by exposing and whipping her in a cart.

cast: cast off.

change: alternation of Fortune.

Chanticleer: the gullible cock in Chaucer's "Nun's Priest's Tale."

character: to write.

check: to rebuke.

cheerly: cheerful, cheerily.

chopped: chapped.

cicatrice: scar, impression.

cipher: zero.

clap into: to begin briskly.

Cleopatra: queen of Egypt, the mistress of Antony.

clown: peasant, jester.

cods: pods, testicles.

color: kind.

compact of: composed of.

compliment: courtesy.

concave: hollow; therefore insincere.

conceit: imagination.

conduct: leadership, command.

constant: uniform (of a color); faithful, certain.

convertite: one who has become religious.

cony: rabbit.

cope: to meet, encounter; to debate with.

cote: cottage.

counter: a worthless coin.

countercheck: rebuff (a figure from chess).

cover: to prepare the table for a meal.

coz: cousin.

credit: reputation.

cross: burden; coin stamped with a cross on one side.

Cupid: Eros, the god of love.

curtle-axe: cutlass, a broad and heavy sword used for cutting instead of stabbing.

damask: striped red and white; the color of the damask rose.

dead shepherd: usually taken as a reference to Christopher Marlowe; Phebe's couplet is a quotation from Marlowe's Ovidian poem *Hero and Leander* (1. 175–176).

dearly: expensively.

defy: reject, disdain.

desert: uninhabited.

Destinies: the Parcae, or Fates, three goddesses believed to control the span of human life.

device: quality of mind.

dial: sundial.

Diana in the fountain: this is perhaps an allusion to the myth of Diana and Acteon. Acteon, a hunter, came upon Diana bathing naked in a fountain. She threw water on him, and he was changed into a stag and devoured by his own hounds. In the Renaissance, the hounds were usually interpreted as Acteon's passions.

disable: disparage, belittle.

discord in the spheres: in Ptolemaic astronomy the spheres revolving around the earth were supposed to produce music. The music of the spheres was a Renaissance symbol of the ordered operation of the universe.

disputable: argumentative; given to argument.

diverted blood: unnatural relationship.

dog-ape: dog-faced baboon.

doom: judgment, sentence.

doublet and hose: short jacket and tights, the ordinary Elizabethan male attire.

ducdame: the meaning of this word is unclear. The most probable explanation is that it is a corruption of the Romani (Gypsy) word for "I foretell, I tell fortunes."

effigies: likenesses, portraits.

elegy: a song of complaint about the sadness of love.

emulator: ambitious or jealous rival.

enchantingly: as if under a magic spell.

engage: to pledge.

envenom: to poison; there is probably a reference here to the shirt of Nessus with which Hercules was poisoned (Ovid, *Metamorphoses* IX, 157–158).

erewhile: a little while ago.

even: clear, plain.

exercise: employment, training.

extent: seizure of lands and property in execution of a writ.

eyne: eyes.

fantasy: desire; imagination.

favor: appearance.

feeder: servant, shepherd.

fell: covering of hair or wool; fleece.

fleet: to pass (time); to let time float past.

flux: discharge.

foil: to throw in wrestling; defeat. Literally, a foil is a setting which sets off the brilliance of a jewel; to "foil" someone, then, means to make him a setting against which one

may appear to better advantage.

fond: foolish.

forked head: an arrow with the points stretched forward.

Fortune: see *housewife Fortune.*

freestone coloured: either the dirty white of limestone or the reddish brown of sandstone.

freshly: healthily, youthfully, vigorously.

friend: relative.

gamester: athlete.

Ganymede: a handsome boy with whom Zeus fell in love and carried to Olympus to be cup-bearer to the gods.

Gargantua: the giant in Rabelais whose mouth was so large that he once swallowed five pilgrims.

gesture: manner, attitude.

go alone: to walk without crutches.

God 'ild you: God reward you.

golden world: in the Renaissance, the Golden Age of classical mythology was associated with the happy and innocent state of the Garden of Eden.

grace: virtue, honor.

gracious: popular, in favor.

graff: to graft.

gravelled: perplexed, nonplused.

Greek: a cheat, a roisterer.

grow upon: to encroach upon.

have with you: I'll come with you.

Helen: wife of Menelaus, king of Sparta. Her abduction by Paris caused the Trojan War.

hem: to clear away with a cough.

Hercules be thy speed: may Hercules help you.

hind: farm servant.

hold intelligence: to communicate.

holla: stop.

holy bread: bread blessed and given after the Mass to those who had not communicated.

honest: chaste, virtuous.

horns: the traditional mark of the cuckold.

housewife Fortune: "housewife" means both a woman who manages a house and a hussy, and Fortune can be seen in both these aspects. The wheel is the traditional emblem of Fortune.

humorous: capricious, whimsical, temperamental.

huntress' name: Rosalind, a young virgin, was naturally dedicated to Diana, the goddess of chastity and the hunt.

hurtling: noise of battle.

hyen: hyena.

Hymen: the god of marriage.

ill-favoredly: in an ugly way.

imbossed: swollen.

incision: engrafting (an operation to cure Corin of his foolishness).

incontinent: immediately; unchaste.

indented: curving, winding.

in despite of: in spite of; without use of.

inland: of the central, and thus more cultured, part of a country.

in little: in miniature.

in respect of: in comparison with.

instance: illustration, example.

intendment: intention.

ipse: he.

jointure: part of a dowry reserved for a widow.

Jove's tree: the oak was sacred to Jove (Jupiter).

Judas: Judas was traditionally supposed to have had red hair.

Juno's swans: the swan is traditionally sacred to Venus, while Juno's bird is the peacock.

justly: exactly, precisely.

kind: nature; way.

kindle: to incite; to bring forth.

knoll: to ring, toll.

Leander: a famous classical lover, the subject of Marlowe's poem, *Hero and Leander*. Each night he swam the Hellespont to visit Hero in Sestos.

learn: to teach.

leer: appearance, complexion.

lie with: to lodge with (be buried); to have sexual intercourse with—hence Orlando's use of the word "modest" in his reply.

limned: portrayed, drawn.

liver: traditionally regarded as the seat of the passions.

look to't: to be careful.

loth: unwilling.

Lucretia: Roman matron who killed herself after having been raped by Sextus Tarquinus. In the Renaissance she became a pattern of womanly virtue.

make: to do.

manage: training of a horse in various gaits.

manners: polite behavior; morals.

Marry: an oath by the Virgin Mary.

material: full of sense; gross.

mean: lowly.

measure: solemn and stately dance.

medlar: a small brown-skinned apple eaten when decayed; with a pun on "meddler."

meed: reward.

mere: absolute.

mettle: character, substance.

mewling: mewing like a cat; whimpering.

mine: to undermine.

misconsters: misconstrues.

misprised: undervalued, despised. Note that Duke Frederick wishes to banish Celia for the same reason Oliver wishes to rid himself of Orlando.

modern: everyday.

moe: more.

moonish: fickle, changeable.

moralize: to interpret morally or symbolically.

mortal: subject to death; common to mankind; (?) excessive.

motley: the parti-colored costume of a fool.

names: from the Latin *nomina*, the names on a note of indebtedness.

napkin: handkerchief.

natural: noun, half-wit; *ad-*

jective, related by blood, tender, kind, half-witted. The ambiguities of this word are important throughout the play.

Nature: the antithesis between Nature and Fortune is common in the Renaissance, the point being that man need not worry about the effects of Fortune if he concerns himself with the natural.

naught: quiet; wicked; worthless, useless.

new-fangled: fond of novelty.

nice: fastidious, delicate, trivial.

nominate: to name.

note: melody.

oblivion: forgetfulness.

occasion: opportunity for finding fault.

odds: advantage, superiority.

'ods: God's.

of: by.

osier: willow.

out: embarrassed by a failure of memory.

painted cloth: cheap wall-hanging, usually painted with sentimental or mythological stories in imitation of tapestry.

pale: fence, enclosure.

pantaloon: a thin and foolish old man who was a stock figure in the Commedia dell'Arte.

pard: leopard or panther.

parlous: perilous, dangerous.

parts: qualities.

penalty of Adam: the cycle of the seasons is supposed to have begun with the Fall of Man. In Eden spring was perpetual.

perforce: by force.

perpend: to consider.

phoenix: unique Arabian bird which dies and is re-created from its own ashes.

point-device: perfectly correct.

poke: pocket, wallet.

policy: craftiness.

politic: cunning, scheming.

practise: to conspire or plot.

presently: immediately.

prime: spring-time; with the secondary meaning of "sexually excited."

priser: prize-fighter.

prodigal portion: a reference to the Biblical story of the Prodigal Son (Luke, 15).

proper: handsome.

public haunt: public resort, society of man.

puisny: inferior, incompetent (pronounced "puny").

purchase: to acquire.

purgation: proof, testing; clearing from accusation or suspicion.

purlieu: land on the border of a forest.

put on: to force something upon one.

Pythagoras: Greek philosopher and mathematician (born about 580 B.C.). In the Renaissance he was thought to have introduced the doctrine of the transmigration of souls.

quail: to fail, slacken.

queen of night: the moon; "thrice-crowned" because the moon is the symbol of the triple goddess Diana-Luna-Hecate.

quintain: a wooden figure to practice tilting with.

quintessence: the "fifth essence," supposed to be the substance of which the heavenly bodies are made; therefore, the purest part of a thing.

quit: to absolve.

quittance: discharge from debt; repayment.

quotidian: a continuous fever.

rank: position; odor.

rankness: rebelliousness, insolence; foulness.

rascal: young, lean or inferior deer.

reck: to care for, mind.

reckoning: bill.

recountment: recital of a story.

religion: strict fidelity.

religious: member of a monastic order.

remorse: pity, tenderness.

resolve: to answer (a question).

reverence: position worthy of respect. Orlando's comment is clearly ironic, thus accounting for the fact that Oliver strikes him.

roynish: scurvy.

sad: serious.

sale-work: ready-made goods, and therefore of a poor quality.

sans: without.

sauce: to rebuke.

scrip and scrippage: a small bag and its contents.

searching: probing.

sequestered: cut off from one's fellows, excommunicated.

shrew: cruel.

simple: ingredient in medicine, herb.

something: somewhat.

sort: class, rank.

spleen: impulse, whim, caprice.

squandering: wandering, random.

stalking-horse: an imitation horse, behind which a fowler hid to get close to the game.

stanzo: stanza.

stays: keeps; with a pun on "sties."

still: always, continually.

successfully: likely to succeed.

suddenly: immediately.

sufference: permission.

suit: request; clothing.

swashing: swaggering.

ta'en up: settled.

tax: to criticize.

taxation: making an accusation or satirical attack; slander.

term: session of a court.

thrasonical: boastful; from Thraso, the braggart warrior in Terence's comedy *Eunuchus.*

thrifty hire: wages saved.

toad: the toad was believed to have a stone in his head from which could be made an antidote to poisons.

Touchstone: the clown's name is derived from the flintlike stone used to test the purity of gold and silver.

Troilus: son of Priam, king of Troy, who was betrayed in love by Cressida. Achilles killed Troilus with a spear, not a club.

trow: to believe, think, know.

turn: adapt, change; to fashion a poem or a song.

umber: brown coloring.

uncouth: strange, wild.

unexpressive: inexpressible.

unquestionable: not inviting conversation.

untuneable: discordant.

use: profit.

vent: to utter.

verge: bank.

videlicet: namely.

warn: to keep, protect.

warp: to shrink or to distort (by freezing); to cause to go astray.

weaker vessel: woman.

wearing: wearying.

weed: to uproot; with a pun on "weeds" as garments.

wintered: exposed to winter.

wit: good sense, wisdom.

withal: with this, with it.

woman of the world: married woman.

working: intention, endeavor.

young: inexperienced.